# EDITH STEIN

### Sister Teresa Benedicta of the Cross
### Discalced Carmelite

# *THE HIDDEN LIFE*

## *HAGIOGRAPHIC ESSAYS*
## *MEDITATIONS*
## *SPIRITUAL TEXTS*

*Translated by Waltraut Stein, Ph.D.*

ICS Publications
Institute of Carmelite Studies
Washington, D.C.
1992

The original of this work was published in German by
Archivum Carmelitanum Edith Stein under the title of (Band XI)
*Verborgenes Leben*
*Hagiographische Essays, Meditationen, Geistliche Texte*
Translation authorized.
© Verlag Herder, Freiburg 1987.
English translation copyright
©Washington Province of Discalced Carmelites, Inc. 1992


ICS Publications
2131 Lincoln Road NE
Washington, DC 20002-1199

*Typeset and produced in the U.S.A.*

**Library of Congress Cataloging-in-Publication Data**

Stein, Edith, 1891-1942.
    [Verborgenes Leben. English]
    The hidden life: hagiographic essays, meditations, spiritual texts /
edited by L. Gelber and Michael Linssen ; translated by Waltraut Stein.
    p.  cm. — (The Collected works of Edith Stein; v. 4)
    Translation of : Verborgenes Leben.
    Includes bibliographical references and index.
    ISBN: 0-935216-17-0
    1. Spiritual Life—Catholic authors.  2. Monastic and religious life of
women—Meditations.  3. Converts from Judaism—Religious life.
4. Carmelites—Religious Life.  5. Christian hagiography.
I. Gelber, Lucy.  II. Linssen, Michael.  III. Title.  IV. Series : Stein, Edith,
1891-1942. Works. English. 1986; v. 4.
B3332.S672E54   1986 vol. 4
[BX2350]
193 s—dc20
[240]

91-32114
CIP

# Contents

# Contents

# Translator's Note

Hidden in a convent and hidden in God during a time when the world around her was caught up in the conflagration ignited by Adolf Hitler, Edith Stein reveals both her awareness of the fire and her vision of the cross rising above it.

The essays in this book, particularly the later ones written while she was a member of the Carmelite community in Echt, Holland, permit a glimpse of the faith and surrender that has led the church to declare this woman blessed.

It has been my privilege and consolation to encounter my great aunt Edith on these pages as I struggled to grasp her thoughts in German and translate them into English. At this time, I want to acknowledge the help of Sr. Josephine Koeppel, O.C.D., in rendering traditional Carmelite ideas and Roman Catholic rites into contemporary idiomatic English. I also want to thank Fr. John Sullivan, O.C.D., and Fr. Steven Payne, O.C.D., for their support and encouragement of this effort. At the same time, I alone take responsibility for any errors that may still remain in this translation.

Waltraut Stein
Atlanta, Georgia

# Preface

The present Volume XI of *Edith Steins Werke* takes the reader into the spiritual-religious world in which Edith Stein, Sister Teresa Benedicta of the Cross, O.C.D., spent the last years of her life. It contains hagiographic essays, meditations, and spiritual texts. Its value in terms of the whole of her works lies mainly in that Edith Stein here makes explicit in various places—occasionally directly but mostly indirectly—something of which she speaks seldom or never in her philosophical works, her autobiography, or her letters: her own inner life.

Those who want to become more closely acquainted with Edith Stein's personality may refer to her letters (Volumes VIII and IX in this series). The works in this eleventh volume are all the more significant because they stem from a time in Edith Stein's life from which very few letters have been preserved.

The autobiography (Volume VII) and the description of the last part of her life by Father Romaeus Leuven, O.C.D., (Volume X) are complemented and deepened by this volume.

This volume was edited by Dr. L. Gelber and by the author of this introduction, who has been allowed to continue the work of Father Romaeus Leuven, who died in 1983 and had worked for decades on the legacy of Edith Stein.

Edith Stein observes and describes in a philosophically grounded objectivity. To be sure, she remains the one who observes and describes and so reveals—even if indirectly—her interior nature.

The last part of her life is stamped by Carmel. So it is no wonder that Edith Stein in her reflections on Carmel, on its history and spirit, its prayer and guiding figures, puts into words insights and experiences that, because of her openness and honesty, also are significant for her own deepest life experiences concerning the relationship to divine life and the "little way," in regard to the church, Carmel, grace, and the cross.

It is no accident that some great female figures are presented and considered in this volume. Nor is it a biased arrangement by the editors. Edith Stein's thoughts on women and on their education are here expressed concretely and as true to life. Edith Stein clearly recognized the uniqueness of women, which motivates the contemporary involvement of women in politics and the life of the church in three respects. Their efforts should not be directed toward having but toward being; not toward possession and power, but toward community and humanity. A

woman's actions should not be based on competition and self-impor-
tance in all areas of her life, but rather on her feminine uniqueness, on
the always personal character of her participation and her interests, on
her striving toward wholeness and completeness, on her personality
created in the image of God. (See *Woman,* Volume V in this series.[1])

Repeatedly Edith Stein writes that what happens interiorly to a
person, in that person's life with God, remains hidden so that no one is
to be informed of it. But she also says that the effects of God's grace
cannot remain hidden. By associating with God the human being grows
toward his or her perfection. In this growing into oneself and toward
God, one inevitably and irrevocably encounters the cross. This is "perhaps a quiet, life-long martyrdom of which no one has any idea," or
more outwardly, "the person zealously striving for God's glory unfail-
ingly evokes bitter opposition to this plan."

Edith Stein saw through the events of the time before and during
World War II. She foresaw the holocaust. She had a premonition of her
end. It was precisely her hiddenness in God that gave her the confident
inner rest and outer composure with which she understood it, to place
it in perspective: "God has not committed himself to leaving us within
the walls of the cloister forever" (14 September 1941). "We do not know
whether we shall see the end of this year" (6 January 1941).

In this volume the *Archivum Carmelitanum Edith Stein* wants not only
to present to readers Edith Stein's conceptions of certain historical de-
velopments, graced persons, and a range of themes concerning the
spiritual life, but also to facilitate a deeper look into the inner spiritual
life of Edith Stein. And, last but not least, to also offer an orientation for
one's own life in the following of Christ.

Michael Linssen, O.C.D.

Geleen Carmel, March 25, 1987

# Editors' Introduction

## I. Selection of the Contributions

Edith Stein was by nature a contemplative person. Without hesitation, she devoted herself to this talent, most truly a part of her nature. At first she followed the pull of God's grace more or less unawares. Then she surrendered to it consciously all the way to giving witness to a lived mysticism.

In the unfolding of her personality, Edith Stein was led on paths of philosophical thinking from phenomenology to the foundations of being. New horizons disclosed themselves to her searching spirit. She recognized the finitude of all created being and so also the mortality of human existence, but at the same time its foundation in an absolute, eternal Being as well. Through the decisive effect of this inner openness, her philosophical path and her secular way of life gradually melded into the character of a contemplative person.

Her search for truth goes hand in hand with her sacrifice of her life, united to the sacrifice on the cross. She lives this search out of a continually fresh enthusiasm and as a member of a universal church.[1] The spiritual fruits of this life's destiny, reflections committed to paper, have a sharp flavor and ripened especially during the time that Edith Stein lived in Carmel.

Edith Stein also had a definite social gift. Above all, she could listen attentively. The apostle James admonished Christians to practice listening: "Everyone should be instantly ready to hear, but be reserved in speaking" (Jas 1:19). Such true listening demands high qualities of char-acter. Genuine listening consists not only in understanding words; it demands of the listener intensive empathy and identification, even going so far as to let oneself be changed to join someone else on the way.

Edith Stein possessed this gift that Gabriel Marcel appropriately calls "creative fidelity," which means making ourselves interiorly open and transparent. Being ready to give, we experience the mysterious reciprocity between free action and ready allowing. So we become participating listeners. It is the meeting of the contemplative and active dispositions of the spirit.[2]

Edith Stein possessed this gift of making inner contact with others even though she herself preferred to remain reserved. What went on in the depths of her soul came out only sparingly. Many who knew her before and after her entrance into the convent attest to this. Her inner life remained *her* secret. But she cannot entirely conceal it from the inquiring eye of posterity. We who are already sufficiently distanced from her in time to listen in on her silence with understanding are permitted to read between the lines of her writings the messages of a soul who had mystical experiences, and probably also a presentiment of the meaning of her life and suffering for posterity.

Considered as a whole, Edith Stein's achievement is a synthesis that is, so to speak, inherently an "ecumenical" effort, synthesizing the philosophy of Thomas Aquinas and the phenomenology of Husserl; blending the Old and New Covenants; creating fellowship among Christian churches; equally valuing men and women; making limited, finite being at home in all-embracing, eternal Being. In her person, Edith Stein herself unites the gifts of rigorous logical thinking and the intuitive flight of the muse, in a seldom-found harmony.

In the comprehensive study of *Finite and Eternal Being*, we encounter not only her philosophical thinking, but also how she broke through the antithesis of spirit and matter to illuminating faith. Freed of enslavement to matter, the human soul can soar up to God.

In the biographies and reflections of this volume, we encounter the spiritual intuition, this invisible divine breath, that led Edith Stein to Carmel where she lived for eight years as Sister Teresa Benedicta of the Cross. Even though the themes of these texts vary a great deal, the author shows that the paths to the religious formation of the human person are nevertheless parallel. Throughout we run into the possibility of the sanctification of the soul's efforts. This possibility becomes an actuality when we freely follow the pull of God's grace and allow ourselves to be led to perfection by God's Spirit. In her descriptions of saints, we see Edith Stein's great gift for psychologically penetrating figures from the past and presenting them as alive. Her clear mind leads her to a faith-filled understanding of an order in all creation by the power of grace.

In summary, we may say that a fourfold goal has determined the selection of the contributions in this volume. The selections endeavor to:

—establish a basis for the origin of Edith Stein's hagiographic essays and her spiritual reflections;
—document Edith Stein's call to Carmel;
—display her thinking in its deepest mystical form;
—bring in the poetic components of Edith Stein's Carmelite spirituality.

This Volume XI of *Edith Steins Werke* in part contains newly revised editions of earlier publications and in part the first publication of manuscripts from her literary estate. The texts originate from the years 1930 to 1942, thus from the turbulent period that begins with Edith Stein's move from Speyer to Münster, and ends shortly before her deportation from the Dutch Carmel in Echt and her death in the gas chambers of Auschwitz.

Even though these manuscripts are often incomplete regarding date and signature, we were able to obtain the missing dates in indirect ways. We can also vouch for the authenticity of the writings with complete certainty.

## II. Origin of the Contributions

Upon entering Carmel, Edith Stein conclusively decided on a religious orientation in her intellectual and spiritual interests. At the same time, however, she saw herself confronting new tasks in her current situation. Thus we find her on the one hand as a mature woman and on the other a young Carmelite. From then on, this tension led to a certain selection of themes.

Since the opportunities for professional work are very limited in the monasteries of the Discalced Carmelites, though one of the possible activities is that of a writer, Sister Benedicta, as Edith Stein was called after her clothing, was asked to compose hagiographic essays and religious reflections on a regular basis.

Along with this mostly exterior reason for the origin of her writings, there also crystallizes an inner, personal motivation: Edith Stein poses and answers questions that are of decisive importance to herself. In the persons and situations that she describes, she frequently recognizes a mirror image of herself, an evident similarity to her own characteristics and experiences. At such points she indirectly breaks her otherwise impenetrable silence about herself. For a moment she lifts the veil behind which her interior life is hidden and permits a glimpse of a vanished yesterday, vanishing today, and dark tomorrow.

## III. Subject Matter of the Contributions

When we take a look at "The Prayer of the Church," we also find answers to the questions of our own time. The spirit that searches more deeply than usual finds here a concisely worded contrast between the prayer and rites of the Old and New Covenants in their factual and historical circumstances. She presents prayer in its dual significance, as divine worship and as an individual dialogue with God. She introduces us to the interior life and so to the prayer life of Carmel and to her own personal prayer life. The maturity, serenity, and religious depth of her words have convincing power.

In "St. Elizabeth of Thuringia," the saint is portrayed enwrapped in fairy-tale magic, as a child of an Hungarian king who resided on the Wartburg, bathed in the light of the legendary fame and brilliance of the nobles of Thuringia. This short biography is simultaneously a verse out of the epic of the German Middle Ages.

In writing "Marie-Aimée de Jésus," about the French Carmelite, Edith Stein paints the picture of a delicate child of angelic purity and spirituality. Born in a thatched hut in a little town in Normandy, she is called from the first day of her life to loving contemplation of the Almighty. This is an episode taken from nineteenth century French devotional life.

In both Elizabeth's and Marie-Aimée's manifest mental attitudes, Edith Stein finds a confirmation of her own knowledge in faith that all creation is directed by the power of grace. In the image of the character of Marie-Aimée she encounters her own self. She cites and comments on texts from their writings,[3] which could also justify her entrance into the Discalced Carmelite Order, could appropriately describe her own intuitive way of working, and present in a true-to-life way her frame of mind as a writer while in the Order.

In the "Sketch of St. Teresa Margaret," Edith Stein talks of the saint's spontaneous empathic ability, a gift that also lent Edith herself unusually strong influential powers and harmoniously united intellect and feelings in her own person.

Two basic thoughts determine Edith Stein's religious form of life. They direct her thinking along religious lines, ground her turning to the contemplative life, and support her activities in the service of the church. One of these is the *love of the cross,* which gives our being, unstable because of change and transience, an ultimate security in the constant primal Ground of eternal Being. The other is *atonement,* which breaks through the disastrous and endless cycle of our own and others' debt of shame in the face of God's goodness and justice and so achieves reconciliation and peace.

Love of the cross and atonement are also expressed in the three vows that regulate monastic life and are ceremonially renewed each year, the vows of poverty, obedience, and celibate chastity.

In Carmel it is customary for the prioress to address her sisters on high feast days of the Order, often about the deepening of prayer life. In the years that Edith Stein spent in the Carmel in Echt, she composed a number of such occasional texts at the request of the superior.[4] In these meditations we hear the voice of a devout soul who in inner abandonment is ready to give up her earthly existence to atone for the outrages of the unchained beast of National Socialism. Above and beyond a violent death without a grave, in these reflections Edith Stein leaves us the moving invitation to live out the conviction of our faith. She breaks her silence to open our inner eye to the "epiphany" of her hidden life.

Finally, we want to mention the providential spiritual relationship of Holy Mother Teresa of Avila to her spiritual daughter Teresa Benedicta of the Cross, a relationship that becomes evident in the hagiographic writing "Love for Love."

In moments of intuitive genius, the human spirit can be elevated to poetic or prophetic vision beyond the limited possibilities of rational insight. In celestial moments of its existence, it may be allotted the grace of temporary rapture into transcendent worlds. Silent meditation is the preparation and the way to comprehensible and incomprehensible elevations of the soul and so to entrance to the ultimate depths of one's own self.

The clear language of prose is suitable for expressing rational thought; meditative and prophetic ascension of the spirit requires the linguistic expression of the poetic form. Words fail in the vision of the transcendent; their place is taken by wordless contemplation in deepest silence.

Between the lines of the writings one can read that the lives of these two women, the saintly Mother Teresa of Avila and Blessed Sister Teresa Benedicta of the Cross, have all along been parallel. Edith Stein went through a decisive upheaval upon reading the life of the Holy Mother. From then on she became profoundly familiar with the prayer life of Carmel, even to the heights of mystical experience before she ever donned a nun's habit. Stepping over the threshold of the monastery meant for her the confirmation and perfection of the lifestyle that suited her best.[5]

## IV. Authenticity of the Edition

This eleventh volume of *Edith Steins Werke* contains thirteen distinct contributions, some of which are short reflections and others long articles, as well as a group of dialogues and poems. The texts are brought together by the editors in book form under the title of *The Hidden Life: Hagiographic Essays, Meditations, Spiritual Texts*.

The individual contributions are not organized chronologically but according to content along the following basic lines: before the face of God; on God's mercy; at the foot of the cross; the grace of vocation. The inclusion of the poems as the last contribution is intended as a presentation of Edith Stein's spiritual perfection and her readiness to give up her life as an atoning sacrifice for fallen humanity. The reader will welcome the opportunity to expand the picture of Edith Stein's personality and her activity as a Discalced Carmelite by perusing the contributions in this suggested order.

The texts of the unpublished essays and reflections were put together partly from ordered, partly from loose manuscript pages, from copies, and from various kinds of documentation. Some of the papers were recovered from the ruins of the monastery in Herkenbosch in the Netherlands.[6] The reconstruction of the texts was done by comparing them with works first published during the author's lifetime, to determine if perhaps we were dealing with manuscript pages of these works. We also examined the paper and the typeface.

The texts of the dialogues and poems are in the Archives of the Carmel in Cologne. Mother Maria Amata Neyer has granted us permission to use them in this volume.[7]

The contributions were revised using the following guidelines (in terms of language and not of content):

—The text has been clearly divided by the uniform placement of the title and subtitles, by the completion of missing inscriptions, and by breaking up overlong sections into additional paragraphs. Sentence structure that was in error or incomplete sentences have been improved according to their sense and occasionally expanded.

—Spelling, punctuation, and sentence structure have been standardized according to current German usages.

—Names in the Old and New Testaments have been written in accord with today's rules, Spanish names presented in their original form.

These changes in the original texts are not mentioned in the notes to the individual manuscripts.

Changes, deletions, or additions by a different hand have been ignored. We are literally reproducing the original wording of the relevant manuscripts. Supplementary notes or remarks by the editors [or occasionally by the translator] are indicated with brackets.


## I.1. *On the History and Spirit of Carmel*

This article appeared with the above title in the Sunday supplement "Zu neuen Ufern," Number 13 of the *Augsburger Postzeitung [Augsburg Post]* on March 31, 1935. The author is designated as Sister Teresia Benedicta a Cruce (Edith Stein). The Cologne Carmel has a photograph of the original newspaper. The *Archivum* has a copy of the article under the call number DI 20, whose text Mother Maria Amata Neyer published in the internal newsletter of German Carmelites, *Treffpunkt [Contact Point]* 6, no. 1 (1976), pp. 13-17.

Paper: 5 single sheets with page numbers 13-17, 28 ½ x 21 cm.
Script: Typewriter.

Cf. a comment in a letter by Edith Stein to Gisela Naegeli on August 9, 1935 (*Edith Steins Werke,* Vol. IX, Letter 209): "The essay appeared on

Laetare Sunday [the fourth Sunday in Lent] in the Sunday supplement of the *Augsburger Postzeitung.*"

## I.2. *The Prayer of the Church*

In the *Archivum* under call number DI 11 are two copies published at that time by the Akademischen Bonifacius-Einigung, Paderborn in its series "Vom Strom des Lebens in der Kirche," single issue 4: Teresia Benedicta a Cruce, O.C.D., "The Prayer of the Church." The issue is undated. The imprimatur on the volume is December 11, 1936, copyright 1937. Along with its own pagination, the installment also contains the pagination of the entire work.

Paper: 16 printed sheets, 23 x 15 ½ cm.

Script: Printed text without handwritten notes in Edith Stein's hand.

Under the call number AII K is page 1 of the handwritten manuscript with the title, *Vom Gebet der Kirche [The Prayer of the Church].* It is a single sheet of paper that Edith Stein used, along with letters from the year 1936, to write summaries of philosophical works.[8] The letters confirm the assumption that the manuscript originated in 1936.

Paper: 1 single sheet, 20 ½ x 16 cm.

Script: Roman script, ink, on one side of the sheet (on the other side philosophical notes).

## II.1. *The Spirit of St. Elizabeth as It Informed Her Life*

The entire manuscript of the article with the above title *[Lebensgestaltung im Geist der heiligen Elisabeth]* is found in the *Archivum* under the call number DI 2 signed with the name Dr. Edith Stein (Breslau).

Paper: 40 single sheets, 21 x 16 ½ cm.

Script: Roman script, ink, writing on one side of the sheets.

The manuscript is undated, but accompanied by a syllabus that links the manuscript with lectures that Edith Stein gave during this time all over the German-speaking world:

Saint Elizabeth
A. Meaning of the Jubilee.
B. I Her external path through life
    II The spirit that speaks from this: love, cheerfulness, naturalness— a strong mystical lifestyle (admonitions of her life, Franciscan spirit, obedience)
    III Nature—freedom—grace as principles informing her life

Paper: 1 double sheet, 15 x 11 cm.

Script: Roman script, ink, written on one side of the sheet.

The article appeared in the *Benediktinischen Monatsschrift* XIII, Nos. 9/10 (1931), pp. 366-377, with slight changes in the text from the manuscript published here. The syllabus remained unpublished, and appears in print for the first time here.

The manuscript reproduces the wording of the lecture that Edith Stein gave on January 24, 1932 in Zürich.[9]

Cf. the printed version of this lecture published by Herderbücherei, No. 129, Freiburg, 1962.

## II.2. *Love for Love*

Found in the *Archivum* under the call number DI 3:

—The complete manuscript of the article with the above title and the addition *Leben und Werke der heiligen Teresa von Jesus* and dated at the end of the foreword: Carmel Cologne-Lindenthal, Candlemas, 1934.

Paper: 67 double sheets and 5 single sheets, 21½ x 17 cm. On the back of the sheets a carbon copy of a typewritten work by Stein: *Des heiligen Thomas von Aquino Untersuchungen über die Wahrheit.*

Script: Roman script, ink, the text of DI 3 written on one side of the sheets.

—A typewritten copy of the manuscript with the author's notes for possible places to shorten it; changes in the title, completion of her name and corrections of the text in an unknown hand.

Paper: 64 single sheets about 15½ x 10½ cm.

Script of the notes: handwritten, ink.

The article appeared in *Kleine Lebensbilder,* No. 84, Freiburg, Kanisiuswerk, 1934.

Edith Stein mentions the appearance of the shortened article in her letter to Mother Petra Brüning of October 17, 1934 (*Edith Steins Werke,* Vol. IX, Letter 182): "I am allowed to send you the little book on Teresa that I wrote for our dear mother's name day and that has now appeared—even though horribly shortened...."

These dates reveal that Edith Stein, still using her name in the world, wrote this study of St. Teresa while she was a postulant, and that this article composed during the first months of her life in the Order appeared in print after her clothing (April 15, 1934), now using her religious name. At that time the original title of the manuscript was also changed to *Teresa of Jesus.*

## II.3. *St. Teresa Margaret of the Sacred Heart*

The complete manuscript of this article is found in the *Archivum* under the call number DI 5 with the above title and with the twofold imprimatur:

—Provincial Office (Ratisbonae, April 25, 1934);

—Episcopal Ordinary (Würzburg, April 28, 1934).

Moreover, the Cologne Carmel is in possession of the document with an imprimatur dated April 6, 1934, in Cologne and signed by Dr. David, Vicar General.

The manuscript is undated and signed "Sister Teresia Benedicta a Cruce O.C.D."; it nevertheless begins with the sentence, "On March 19, 1934 Pope Pius XI entered Blessed Teresa Margaret of the Heart of Jesus in the register of saints."

Paper: 17 double sheets and 1 single sheet, 21 ½ x 17 cm. On the back of the sheets a carbon copy of a typewritten work by Stein: *Des heiligen Thomas von Aquino Untersuchungen über die Wahrheit.*

Script: Roman script, ink, sheets inscribed on one side with the text of DI 5.

The article was published by Rita-Verlag, Würzburg, 1934.

From these dates it can be concluded that Edith Stein conceived this article, too, in the year of her clothing and reworked it for publication.

## II.4. *A Chosen Vessel of Divine Wisdom*

Found in the *Archivum* under the call number DI 9:

—The complete manuscript of the essay with the above title and the subtitle: *Sr. Marie-Aimée de Jésus of the Carmel of the Avenue de Saxe in Paris, 1839-1874.* The manuscript is signed by Edith Stein using the name "Sr. Teresia Benedicta a Cruce, Karmel Echt," though undated.

Paper: 9 double sheets, 23 x 14 ½ cm.

Script: Roman script, ink. Writing on both sides of the sheets.

—A carefully corrected typewritten copy signed by Edith Stein using the name "Sr. Teresia Benedicta a Cruce O.C.D.," but also undated.

Paper: 22 single sheets, 27 ½ x 21 ½ cm.

Script of the revision: Roman script, ink.

—A photocopy of a second sample of this typewritten version that remained in the Carmel in Echt with a handwritten dedication to the then prioress, Mother Ottilia Thammisch. The dedication reads, "To Dear Reverend Mother Ottilia on September 29, 1940 in filial love and gratitude. Sr. Teresia Benedicta a Cruce."

The manuscript, unpublished until now, appears in print here for the first time. References to this study can be found in Edith Stein's correspondence; see *Edith Steins Werke,* Vol. IX:

—First in writing to Sr. Marie Agnella Stadtmüller, O.P., on October 29, 1939 (Letter 306): "Recently, I finished a little biography of the Carmelite Marie-Aimée de Jésus (of the Paris Carmel) for a collection that Fr. Eugen Lense is publishing with Benziger."

—One year later in a letter to Mother Johanna van Weersth, O.C.D., (Letter 316): "I am sending Your Reverence a little biography of Sr. Marie-Aimée. I wrote it more than a year ago for a collection that was supposed to come out around Easter. But now it cannot be published before the end of the war. In any case, Sr. M. Electa will be interested in it. Her translation, which we read at table, led me to choose M.-Aimée when I was asked for a portrait of a Carmelite."

On the basis of these indications, we can assume that the study was done in 1939 for publication by Benziger, Einsiedeln,[10] but did not appear in print at that time because of the war.


## III.1. *Love of the Cross*

In the *Archivum* under the call number DI 6 there is a typewritten copy of this article with the above title and the subtitle: *For the Feast of St. John of the Cross.* The copy is originally signed by Edith Stein with the name "Dr. Edith Stein," later supplemented by her religious name: "Schw. Teresia Benedicta a Cruce, Köln-Lindenthal."

In an unknown hand, assumed to be that of someone from the Carmel in Echt, the addition Köln-Lindenthal was crossed out. Also, along with other words crossed out in the text, the wording of the title was changed to "Mystical Expiatory Suffering: For the Feast of St. John of the Cross, November 24." The reader will find here the original, unabridged version of the text.

The reflection is undated, but presumably written around 1934 after her entrance into the Carmel of Cologne.

Paper: 3 1/2 single sheets, 29 1/2 x 21 cm.

Signature: Roman script, ink.

The article appears in print here for the first time.


## III.2. *Elevation of the Cross*

The complete manuscript of this meditation is found in the *Archivum* under the call number DI 12 with the above title, and the subtitle: *Sep-*

*tember 14, 1939: Ave Crux, Spes Unica.* The text is not signed.

Since Edith Stein came to Echt on New Year's Eve, 1938, these pages were written for the community there during the first year of her stay in the Echt Carmel, for its yearly renewal of vows on the feast of the Exaltation of the Cross (September 14).

Paper: 2 double sheets, 24½ x 14½ cm.

Script: Roman script, ink, written on both sides of the sheets.

The text appears in print here for the first time.

### III.3. *The Marriage of the Lamb*

The complete manuscript of these reflections with the above title is found in the *Archivum* under the call number DI 10, with the subtitle: *For September 14, 1940.* The text is not signed.

Thus, these reflections were written in the following year, also for the convent family (see above, III.2).

Paper: 8 double sheets, 24½ x14½ cm.

Script: Roman script, ink, written on both sides of some pages and on one side of others.

The text is published here for the first time.

### III.4. *Exaltation of the Cross*

The complete manuscript of this third meditation for September 14 is found in the *Archivum* under the call number DI 15 with the above title and the subtitle: *September 9, 1941.* The text is not signed.

Thus, welling from the deepest depths, this exhortation for the Exaltation of the Cross dates from the third and last year Edith Stein was permitted to spend still under the protective roof of the Carmel in Echt (deportation: August 1942). The meditation clearly has to do with the vows of the Order and their renewal on the feast of the Exaltation of the Cross; therefore, it was intended as an address by the Mother Prioress on this solemn feast day (see above, III.2 and III.3).

Paper: 2 double sheets, 22 x 17 cm.

Script: Roman script, ink, written on two sides of the sheets.

The text appears in print here for the first time.

### IV.1. *Three Addresses*

Like the previous reflections (see III.1-4), these texts were also conceived as addresses and lectures by the prioress. The first text was for the clothing of a novice, and the two following texts were for the then customary renewal of vows in the Carmelite Order at Epiphany (January 6).

### a. For the First Profession of Sister Miriam of Little St. Thérèse

The complete manuscript of this spiritual address is found in the *Archivum* under the call number DI 13, with the above title and the subtitle: *July 16, 1940.* The text is not signed.

By teaching Latin in the novitiate in Echt (see *Edith Steins Werke,* Vol. X, Ch. 7), Edith Stein had a strong influence on the formation of the young sisters. Sister Miriam was one of the novices who attended Edith Stein's daily classes.

Paper: 6 single sheets, 21 ½ x 16 cm.

Script: Roman script, ink, written on two sides of the sheet.

The text appears in print here for the first time.

### b. The Hidden Life and Epiphany

The complete manuscript for this meditation for the Feast of the Three Wise Men from the East is found in the *Archivum* under the call number DI 16. The text is neither signed nor dated.

Since Edith Stein came to Echt in 1938 and since there are two additional reflections for the Feast of the Three Kings in the *Archivum,* one for the year 1941, the other for the year 1942,[11] the present manuscript can be dated January 6, 1940 with certainty.

The text appears in print here for the first time.

### c. For January 6, 1941

The complete manuscript of this second meditation for the end of the Christmas liturgical cycle is found in the *Archivum* under the call number DI 14. The text is not signed.

Paper: 2 double sheets, 22 x 14 cm.

Script: Roman script, ink, written on two sides of the sheets.

The text appears in print here for the first time.

## IV.2. *Three Dialogues*

In the *Archivum* there are only photocopies of typewritten manuscripts, under the call numbers DI 22, 23, and 24, of these dramatic and oral pieces whose texts Mother Johanna van Weersth gave to the Cologne Carmel in later years along with precise statements. At this point we express our heartfelt thanks to Mother Johanna a Cruce.

Possibly Edith Stein's written copies of these three pieces of fiction have been lost, or perhaps may still be found later. These manuscripts were not presented to Fr. Romaeus Leuven, O.C.D., when he visited the Dutch Discalced Carmelites as provincial and examiner of Edith Stein's writings at the Carmel in Echt.

The dialogues are occasional pieces in two respects. They were conceived as presentations for specific feast days of the monastic community and were acted out and presented by the novitiate as "stage plays." At the same time, they are implicitly the written record of thoughts springing from the hiddenness of the deepest interiority: illuminations of her own path of seeking and finding the truth that led to her conversion and baptism; the meaning of the fate of the Jews; and, furthermore, Edith Stein's motivation for her own religious calling.

The composition of the fictional pieces in dialogue form and metrical language display a basic characteristic of Edith Stein's literary talents. Already in her youth she used to write dramatic and oral pieces, related concretely to the occasion, for celebrations with family and friends; see, among other texts, *Edith Steins Werke,* Vol. VII, (complete edition, 1985), pp. 102, 146, 149, 184. In later years, she once again seized on the dialogue form for her initial conception of the comparison of Husserl's phenomenology and the philosophy of St. Thomas Aquinas; see *Edith Steins Werke,* Vol. X, pp. 54 and 56.

### *a. I Am Always in Your Midst*

This dialogue, first in time, was presented for Mother Ottilia's name day on December 13, 1939.

The discourse of Mother Ursula with St. Angela, the foundress of the Ursuline congregation, has to do with Mother Petra Brüning, Superior of the Ursulines in Dorsten, and their concern and doubt about their work at that time as guides of young souls (see *Edith Steins Werke,* Vol. IX, Letter 321).

Paper: 3 single sheets, 29 ½ x 21 cm.

Script: Neither edited nor signed in Edith Stein's hand.

An original copy of the manuscript (in the possession of the Cologne Carmel) bears the above title and says that Edith Stein wrote on 6 sheets double-spaced and double-sided, that she folded these in half, bound them together with a thread, and numbered the pages from 1-11.

The text appears in print here for the first time.

### *b. Te Deum Laudamus: For December 7, 1940 [Feast of St. Ambrose]*

Sister Benedicta wrote this dialogue second (DI 23), for the name day of the newly elected Mother Antonia, whose middle name was Ambrosia.

Paper: 4 single sheets, 29 ½ x 21 cm.
Script: Neither edited nor signed in Edith Stein's hand.
The text appears in print here for the first time.

### c. Conversation at Night

The occasion for this third and last dialogue (DI 24) was the birthday celebration of Mother Antonia on June 13, 1941.[12]

In the dialogue between the prioress and Esther, Edith Stein points as a visionary to the possible deliverance of the Jewish people by the saving power of the cross. She lets Mother Antonia a Spiritu Sancto, the prioress of the Carmel in Echt at that time, and her fellow sisters recognize the crucial significance of constant prayer, and so recognize that all their vocations help with the work of salvation.

Paper: 4 single sheets, 29 ½ x 21 cm.
Script: Neither edited nor signed in Edith Stein's hand.
The text appears in print here for the first time.

## Closing Hymn: Two Poems

### a. I Will Remain With You

In the *Archivum* there is a photocopy of the handwritten script under the call number EIII 3.1. The original is in the Carmel "Maria vom Frieden" in Cologne. The poem is neither dated nor signed. Most likely it originated for the occasion of the departure from the Carmel Köln-Lindenthal on December 31, 1938.

Paper: 3 double sheets 17 ½ x 11 cm.

Script: Roman script, ink, some sheets with writing on one side and some on both sides; two small symbolic drawings at the beginning and the end of the poem.

The text appears in print here for the first time.

### b. And I Remain With You

A typewritten copy of this poem is found in the *Archivum* under the call number EIII 3.2 with improvements in the wording that Fr. Romaeus Leuven, O.C.D., made by comparing it with the handwritten manuscript. The manuscript remained in the Carmel in Echt.

This copy has the inserted comment "(From a Pentecost novena)" over the above title; and under the title in Mother Antonia's handwriting, well-known to us, there is the addition: "Poem after a conversation of ours in the garden. Summer, 1942."

On the basis of this addition dated by Mother Antonia, we may assume that we have here one of Edith Stein's very last poems. We tried to make the breaks of the lines into stanzas more uniform, to improve the indications of sentence endings according to the meaning, but to reproduce the text of the poem word for word.

Paper: 2 single sheets, 29 ½ x 21 cm.

Script: Neither edited nor signed in Edith Stein's hand.

The poem appears in print here for the first time.

Dr. L. Gelber

# I

# *Before the Face of God*

## I.1. On the History and Spirit of Carmel

U ntil a few years ago, very little from our silent monasteries penetrated into the world. It is different today. People talk a lot about Carmel and want to hear something about life behind the high walls. This is chiefly attributable to the great saints of our time who have captivated the entire Catholic world with amazing speed, for instance, *St. Thérèse of the Child Jesus.*[1] Gertrud von le Fort's novel about Carmel[2] has vigorously directed German intellectual circles to our Order, as has her beautiful foreword to the letters of Marie Antoinette de Geuser.[3]

What does the average Catholic know about Carmel? That it is a very strict, perhaps the strictest penitential order, and that from it comes the holy habit of the Mother of God, the brown scapular, which unites many of the faithful in the world to us. The whole church celebrates with us the patronal feast of our Order, the feast of the scapular, on July 16. Most people also recognize at least the names of "little" Thérèse and "great" Teresa, whom we call our Holy Mother. She is generally seen as the founder of the Discalced Carmelites. The person who is a little more familiar with the history of the church and monasteries certainly knows that we revere the prophet Elijah as our leader and father. But people consider this a "legend" that does not mean very much. We who live in Carmel and who daily call on our Holy Father Elijah in prayer know that for us he is not a shadowy figure out of the dim past. His spirit is active among us in a vital tradition and determines how we live. Our Holy Mother strenuously denied that she was founding a new Order. She wanted nothing except to reawaken the original spirit of the old Rule [of St. Albert].

Our Holy Father Elijah succinctly says what is most important in the first words of his that the Scriptures give us. He says to King Ahab who worshiped idols (1 Kgs 17:1), "As the Lord the God of Israel lives, before whom I stand, there shall be neither dew nor rain these years, except by my word."

To stand before the face of the living God—that is our vocation. The

1

holy prophet set us an example. He stood before God's face because this was the eternal treasure for whose sake he gave up all earthly goods. He had no house; he lived wherever the Lord directed him from moment to moment: in loneliness beside the brook of Carith, in the little house of the poor widow of Zarephath of Sidon, or in the caves of Mount Carmel. His clothing was an animal hide like that of that other great penitent and prophet, the Baptist. The hide of a dead animal reminds us that the human body is also subject to death.[4] Elijah is not concerned about his daily bread. He lives trusting in the solicitude of the heavenly Father and is marvelously sustained. A raven brings him his daily food while he is in solitude. The miraculously increased provisions of the pious widow nourish him in Zarephath. Prior to the long trek to the holy mountain where the Lord was to appear to him, an angel with heavenly bread strengthens him. So he is for us an example of the gospel poverty that we have vowed, an authentic prototype of the Savior.

Elijah stands before God's face because all of his love belongs to the Lord. He lives outside all natural human relationships. We hear nothing of his father and mother, nothing of a wife or child. His "relatives" are those who do the will of the Father as he does: Elisha, whom God has designated as his successor, and the "sons of the prophets," who follow him as their leader. Glorifying God is his joy. His zeal to serve God tears him apart: "I am filled with jealous zeal for the Lord, the God of hosts" (1 Kgs 19:10, 14; these words were used as a motto on the shield of the Order). By living penitentially, he atones for the sins of his time. The offense that the misguided people give to the Lord by their manner of worship hurts him so much that he wants to die. And the Lord consoles him only as he consoles his especially chosen ones: He himself appears to Elijah on a lonely mountain, reveals himself in soft rustling after a thunderstorm, and announces his will to him in clear words.

The prophet, who serves the Lord in complete purity of heart and completely stripped of everything earthly, is also a model of obedience. He stands before God's face like the angels before the eternal throne, awaiting God's sign, always ready to serve. Elijah has no other will than the will of his Lord. When God bids, he goes before the king and fearlessly risks giving him bad news that must arouse the king's hatred. When God wills it, he leaves the country at the threat of violence; but he also returns at God's command, though the danger has not disappeared.

Anyone who is so unconditionally faithful to God can also be certain of God's faithfulness. He is permitted to speak "as someone who has power," may open and close heaven, may command the waters to let him walk through and remain dry, may call down fire from heaven to consume his sacrifice, to execute punishment on God's enemies, and may breathe new life into a dead person. We see the Savior's predecessor provided with all the graces that he has promised to his own. And the greatest crown is still in reserve for Elijah: Before the eyes of his true disciple, Elisha, he is carried off in a fiery carriage to a secret place far from all human abodes. According to the testimony of the Book of Revelation, he will return near the end of the world to suffer a martyr's death for his Lord in the battle against the Antichrist.

On his feast, which we celebrate on July 20, the priest goes to the altar in red vestments. On this day the monastery of our friars on Mount Carmel, the site of Elijah's grotto, is the goal of mighty bands of pilgrims. Jews, Moslems, and Christians of all denominations vie in honoring the great prophet. We remember him in the liturgy on still another day, in the epistle and preface of the *Feast of Mount Carmel,* as we usually call the feast of the scapular. On this day we give thanks that our dear Lady has clothed us with the "garment of salvation." The events providing the occasion for this feast did not occur until much later in the Western world. In the year 1251 [according to tradition] the Blessed Virgin appeared to the general of the Order, Simon Stock, an Englishman, and gave him the scapular.[5] But the preface reminds us that it was our dear Lady of Mount Carmel who bestowed this visible sign of her motherly protection on her children far from the original home of the Order. It was she who manifested herself to the prophet Elijah in the form of a little rain cloud and for whom the sons of the prophets built the first shrine on Mount Carmel. The legend of the Order tells us that the Mother of God would have liked to remain with the hermit brothers on Mount Carmel. We can certainly understand that she felt drawn to the place where she had been venerated through the ages and where the holy prophet had lived in the same spirit that also filled her from the time her earthly sojourn began. Released from everything earthly, to stand in worship in the presence of God, to love him with her whole heart, to beseech his grace for sinful people, and in atonement to substitute herself for these people, as the maidservant of the Lord to await his beckoning—this was her life.

The hermits of Carmel lived as sons of the great prophet and as "brothers of the Blessed Virgin." St. Berthold organized them as cenobites, and at the instigation of St. Brocard, the spirit they had received from their predecessors was laid down in our holy *Rule.* Around 1200, it was given to the Order by St. Albert, the patriarch of Jerusalem, and authorized by Pope Innocent IV in 1247.[6] It also condenses the entire meaning of our life in a short statement: "All are to remain in their own cells..., meditating on the Law of the Lord day and night and watching in prayer, unless otherwise justly employed." "To watch in prayer"—this is to say the same thing that Elijah said with the words, "to stand before the face of God." Prayer is looking up into the face of the Eternal. We can do this only when the spirit is awake in its innermost depths, freed from all earthly occupations and pleasures that numb it. Being awake in body does not guarantee this consciousness, nor does the rest required by nature interfere. "To meditate on the Law of the Lord"—this can be a form of prayer when we take prayer in its usual broad sense. But if we think of "watching in prayer" as being immersed in God, which is characteristic of contemplation, then meditation on the Law is only a means to contemplation.

What is meant by "the Law of the Lord"? Psalm 118, which we pray every Sunday and on solemnities at Prime, is entirely filled with the command to know the Law and to be led by it through life. The Psalmist was certainly thinking of the Law of the Old Covenant. Knowing it actually did require life-long study, and fulfilling it, life-long exertion of the will. But the Lord has freed us from the yoke of this Law. We can consider the Savior's great commandment of love, which he says includes the whole Law and the Prophets, as the Law of the New Covenant. Perfect love of God and of neighbor can certainly be a subject worthy of an entire lifetime of meditation. But we understand the Law of the New Covenant, even better, to be the Lord himself, since he has in fact lived as an example for us of the life we should live. We thus fulfill our Rule when we hold the image of the Lord continually before our eyes in order to make ourselves like him. We can never finish studying the Gospels.

But we have the Savior not only in the form of reports of witnesses to his life. He is present to us in the most Blessed Sacrament. The hours of adoration before the Highest Good, and listening for the voice of the eucharistic God, are simultaneously "meditation on the Law of the Lord" and "watching in prayer." But the highest level is reached "when the Law is deep within our hearts" (Ps 40:8), when we are so united with the triune God, whose temple we are, that his Spirit rules all we do or omit. Then it does not mean we are forsaking the Lord when we do the work that obedience requires of us. Work is unavoidable as long as we are subject to nature's laws and to the necessities of life. And, following the word and example of the apostle Paul, our holy Rule commands us to earn our bread by the work of our hands. But for us this work is always merely a means and must never be an end in itself. To stand before the face of God continues to be the real content of our lives.

Islam's conquest of the Holy Land drove the hermit brothers from Carmel. Only for the past 300 years has our Order again had a shrine of the Mother of God on the holy mountain. The transition from solitude into the everyday life of Western culture led to a falsification of the original spirit of the Order. The protective walls of separation, of rigorous penance and of silence fell, and the pleasures and cares of the world pressed through the opened gates. The Monastery of the Incarnation in Avila, which our Holy Mother entered in the year 1535, was such a monastery of the mitigated Rule. For decades she endured the conflict between the snares of worldly relationships and the pull of undivided surrender to God. But the Lord allowed her no rest until she let go of everything that bound her and really became serious about recognizing that *God alone suffices.*

The great schism of faith that was tearing Europe apart during her time, the loss of so many souls, aroused in her the passionate desire to stop the harm and to offer the Lord recompense, whereupon God gave her the idea of taking a little flock of selected souls and founding a monastery according to the original Rule and of serving him there with the greatest perfection. After innumerable battles and difficulties, she was able to found the monastery of St. Joseph in Avila. Her great work of reform grew from there. At her death she left behind 36 monasteries of women and men of the strict observance, the new branch of the Order, the "Discalced" Carmelites. The monasteries of the reform were to be places where the spirit of the ancient Carmel was to live again. The reestablished original Rule and the Constitutions drawn up by the saint herself form the fence by means of which she intended to protect her vineyards against the dangers from without. Her writings on prayer, the most complete and most animated presentation of the inner life, are the precious legacy through which her spirit continues to work among us.[7] (I have published a very concise presentation of her life in the collection "Kleine Lebensbilder" [Freiburg (Switzerland): Kanisiuswerkes, 1934].) It is the ancient spirit of Carmel. However, influenced by the battles over faith raging in her time, she gave stronger emphasis than did the primitive Carmel to the thought of reparation and of supporting the servants of the church who withstood the enemy in the front lines.

As our second father and leader, we revere the first male discalced Carmelite of the reform, St. John of the Cross. We find in him the ancient eremitical spirit in its purest form. His life gives an impression as though he had no inner struggles. Just as from his earliest childhood he was under the special protection of the Mother of God, so from the time he reached the age of reason, he was drawn to rigorous penance, to solitude, to letting go of everything earthly, and to union with God. He was the instrument chosen to be an example and to teach the reformed Carmel the spirit of Holy Father Elijah. Together with Mother Teresa, he spiritually formed the first generation of male and female discalced Car-melites, and through his writings,[8] he also illumines for us the way on the "Ascent of Mount Carmel."

The daughters of St. Teresa, personally trained by her and Father John, founded the first monasteries of the reform in France and Belgium. From there the Order also soon advanced into the Rhineland. The great French Revolution and the Kulturkampf in Germany tried to suppress it by force. But as soon as the pressure abated, it sprang to life again. It was in this garden that the "little white flower" [i.e., St. Thérèse of Lisieux] bloomed, so quickly captivating hearts far beyond the boundaries of the Order, not only as a worker of miracles for those in need, but also as a director of "little souls" on the path of "spiritual childhood." Many people came to know of this path through her, but very few know that it is not really a new discovery, but the path onto which life in Carmel pushes us. The greatness of the young saint was that she recognized this path with ingenious deduction and that she followed it with heroic decisiveness to the end. The walls of our monasteries enclose a narrow space. To erect the structure of holiness in it, one must dig deep and build high, must descend into the depths of the dark night of one's own nothingness in order to be raised up high into the sunlight of divine love and compassion.

Not every century produces a work of reform as powerful as that of our Holy Mother. Nor does every age give us a reign of terror during which we have the opportunity to lay our heads on the executioner's block for our faith and for the ideal of our Order as did the sixteen Carmelites of Compiegne. But all who enter Carmel must give themselves wholly to the Lord. Only one who values her little place in the choir before the tabernacle more highly than all the splendor of the world can live here, can then truly find a joy that no worldly splendor has to offer.

Our daily schedule ensures us of hours for solitary dialogue with the Lord, and these are the foundation of our life. Together with priests and other ancient orders of the church, we pray the Liturgy of the Hours, and this Divine Office is for us as for them our first and most sacred duty. But it is not for us the supporting ground. No human eye can see what God does in the soul during hours of inner prayer. It is grace upon grace. And all of life's other hours are our thanks for them.

Carmelites can repay God's love by their everyday lives in no other way than by carrying out their daily duties faithfully in every respect—all the little sacrifices that a regimen structured day after day in all its details demands of an active spirit; all the self-control that living in close proximity with different kinds of people continually requires and that is achieved with a loving smile; letting no opportunity go by for serving others in love. Finally, crowning this is the personal sacrifice that the Lord may impose on the individual soul. This is the "little way," a bouquet of insignificant little blossoms that are daily placed before the Almighty—perhaps a silent, life-long martyrdom that no one suspects and that is at the same time a source of deep peace and hearty joyousness and a fountain of grace that bubbles over everything—we do not know where it goes, and the people whom it reaches do not know from whence it comes.

Edith on her Clothing Day (April 15, 1934) in the Cologne Carmel, when she took the religious name "Teresa Benedicta of the Cross, O.C.D."

# I.2. The Prayer of the Church

"Through him, with him, and in him in the unity of the Holy Spirit, all honor and glory is yours, Almighty Father, for ever and ever." With these solemn words, the priest ends the eucharistic prayer at the center of which is the mysterious event of the consecration. These words at the same time encapsulate the prayer of the church: honor and glory to the triune God through, with, and in Christ. Although the words are directed to the Father, all glorification of the Father is at the same time glorification of the Son and of the Holy Spirit. Indeed, the prayer extols the majesty that the Father imparts to the Son and that both impart to the Holy Spirit from eternity to eternity.

All praise of God is *through, with,* and *in* Christ. *Through* him, because only through Christ does humanity have access to the Father and because his existence as God-man and his work of salvation are the fullest glorification of the Father; *with* him, because all authentic prayer is the fruit of union with Christ and at the same time buttresses this union, and because in honoring the Son one honors the Father and vice versa; *in* him, because the praying church is Christ himself, with every individual praying member as a part of his Mystical Body, and because the Father is in the Son and the Son the reflection of the Father, who makes his majesty visible. The dual meanings of *through, with,* and *in* clearly express the God-man's mediation.

The prayer of the church is the prayer of the ever-living Christ. Its prototype is Christ's prayer during his human life.

## 1. The Prayer of the Church as Liturgy and Eucharist

The Gospels tell us that Christ prayed the way a devout Jew faithful to the law prayed.[1] Just as he made pilgrimages to Jerusalem at the prescribed times with his parents as a child, so he later journeyed to the temple to celebrate the high feasts there with his disciples. Surely he sang with holy enthusiasm along with his people the exultant hymns in which the pilgrim's joyous anticipation streamed forth: "I rejoiced when I heard them say: Let us go to God's house" (Ps 122:1). From his last supper with his disciples, we know that Jesus said the old blessings over bread, wine, and the fruits of the earth, as they are prayed to this day.[2] So he fulfilled one of the most sacred religious duties: the ceremonial

Passover seder to commemorate deliverance from slavery in Egypt. And perhaps this very gathering gives us the most profound glimpse into Christ's prayer and the key to understanding the prayer of the church.

> While they were at supper, he took bread, said the blessing, broke the bread, and gave it to his disciples, saying, "Take this, all of you, and eat it: this is my body which will be given up for you."
>
> In the same way, he took the cup, filled with wine. He gave you thanks, and giving the cup to his disciples, said, "Take this, all of you, and drink from it: this is the cup of my blood, the blood of the new and everlasting covenant. It will be shed for you and for all so that sins may be forgiven."[3]

Blessing and distributing bread and wine were part of the Passover rite. But here both receive an entirely new meaning. This is where the life of the church begins. Only at Pentecost will it appear publicly as a Spirit-filled and visible community. But here at the Passover meal the seeds of the vineyard are planted that make the outpouring of the Spirit possible. In the mouth of Christ, the old blessings become life-giving words. The fruits of the earth become his body and blood, filled with his life. Visible creation, which he entered when he became a human being, is now united with him in a new, mysterious way. The things that serve to sustain human life are fundamentally transformed, and the people who partake of them in faith are transformed too, drawn into the unity of life with Christ and filled with his divine life. The Word's life-giving power is bound to the sacrifice. The Word became flesh in order to surrender the life he assumed, to offer himself and a creation redeemed by his sacrifice in praise to the Creator. Through the Lord's last supper, the Passover meal of the Old Covenant is converted into the Easter meal of the New Covenant: into the sacrifice on the cross at Golgotha and those joyous meals between Easter and Ascension when the disciples recognized the Lord in the breaking of bread, and into the sacrifice of the Mass with Holy Communion.

As the Lord took the cup, he gave thanks. This recalls the words of blessing thanking the Creator. But we also know that Christ used to give thanks when, prior to a miracle, he raised his eyes to his Father in heaven.[4] He gives thanks because he knows in advance that he will be heard. He gives thanks for the divine power that he carries in himself and by means of which he will demonstrate the omnipotence of the Creator to human eyes. He gives thanks *for* the work of salvation that he is permitted to accomplish, and *through* this work, which is in fact itself the glorification of the triune Godhead, because it restores this Godhead's distorted image to pure beauty. Therefore the whole perpetual sacrificial offering of Christ—at the cross, in the holy Mass, and in the eternal glory of heaven—can be conceived as a single great thanksgiving—as

Eucharist: as gratitude for creation, salvation, and consummation. Christ presents himself in the name of all creation, whose prototype he is and to which he descended to renew it from the inside out and lead it to perfection. But he also calls upon the entire created world itself, united with him, to give the Creator the tribute of thanks that is his due. Some understanding of this eucharistic character of prayer had already been revealed under the Old Covenant. The wondrous form of the tent of meeting, and later, of Solomon's temple, erected as it was according to divine specifications, was considered an image of the entire creation, assembled in worship and service around its Lord. The tent around which the people of Israel camped during their wanderings in the wilderness was called the "home of God among us" (Ex 38:21). It was thought of as a "home below," in constrast to a "higher home."[5] "O Lord, I love the house where you dwell, the place where your glory abides," sings the Psalmist (Ps 26:8), because the tent of meeting is "valued as much as the creation of the world." As the heavens in the creation story were stretched out like a carpet, so carpets were prescribed as walls for the tent. As the waters of the earth were separated from the waters of the heavens, so the curtain separated the Holy of Holies from the outer rooms. The "bronze" sea is modeled after the sea that is contained by its shores. The seven-branched light in the tent stands for the heavenly lights. Lambs and birds stand for the swarms of life teeming in the water, on the earth, and in the air. And as the earth is handed over to people, so in the sanctuary there stands the high priest "who is purified to act and to serve before God." Moses blessed, anointed, and sanctified the completed house as the Lord blessed and sanctified the work of his hands on the seventh day. The Lord's house was to be a witness to God on earth just as heaven and earth are witnesses to him (Dt 30:19).

In place of Solomon's temple, Christ has built a temple of living stones, the communion of saints. At its center, he stands as the eternal high priest; on its altar he is himself the perpetual sacrifice. And, in turn, the whole of creation is drawn into the "liturgy," the ceremonial worship service: the fruits of the earth as the mysterious offerings, the flowers and the lighted candlesticks, the carpets and the curtain, the ordained priest, and the anointing and blessing of God's house. Not even the cherubim are missing. Fashioned by the hand of the artist, the visible forms stand watch beside the Holy of Holies. And, as living copies of them, the "monks resembling angels"[6] surround the sacrificial altar and make sure that the praise of God does not cease, as in heaven so on earth. The solemn prayers they recite as the resonant mouth of the church frame the holy sacrifice. They also frame, permeate, and consecrate all other "daily work," so that prayer and work become a single *opus Dei*, a single "liturgy." Their readings from the holy Scriptures and from the fathers, from the menologies of the church and the teachings of its principal pastors, are a great, continually swelling hymn of praise to the rule of providence and to the progressive actualization of the eternal plan of salvation. Their morning hymns of praise call all of creation together to unite once more in praising the Lord: mountains and hills, streams and rivers, seas and lands and all that inhabit them, clouds and winds, rain and snow, all peoples of the earth, every class and race of people, and finally also the inhabitants of heaven, the angels and the saints. Not only in representations giving them human form and made by human hands are they to participate in the great Eucharist of creation, but they are to be involved as personal beings—or better, we are to unite ourselves through our liturgy to their eternal praise of God.

"We" here refers not just to the religious who are called to give solemn praise to God, but to all Christian people. When these stream into cathedrals and chapels on holy days, when they joyously participate daily in worship using the "people's choral Mass" and the new "folk Mass" forms, they show that they are conscious of their calling to praise God. The liturgical unity of the heavenly with the earthly church, both of which thank God "through Christ," finds its most powerful expression in the preface and Sanctus of the Mass. However, the liturgy leaves no doubt that we are not yet full citizens of the heavenly Jerusalem, but pilgrims on the way to our eternal home. We must always prepare ourselves before we may dare to lift our eyes to the luminous heights and to unite our voices with the "holy, holy, holy" of the heavenly chorus. Each created thing to be used in the worship service must be withdrawn from its profane use, must be purified and consecrated. Before the priest climbs the steps to the altar, he must cleanse himself by acknowledging his sins, and the faithful must do so with him. Prior to each step as the offertory continues, he must repeat his plea for the forgiveness of sins— for himself and for those gathered around him as well as for all to whom the fruits of the sacrifice are to flow. The sacrifice itself is a sacrifice of expiation that transforms the faithful as it transforms the gifts, unlocks heaven for them, and enables them to sing a hymn of praise pleasing to God. All that we need to be received into the communion of saints is summed up in the seven petitions of the Our Father, which the Lord did not pray in his own name, but to instruct us. We say it before communion, and when we say it sincerely and from our hearts and receive communion in the proper spirit, it fulfills all our petitions. Communion delivers us from evil, because it cleanses us of sin and gives us peace of heart that takes away the sting of all other "evils." It brings us the forgiveness of past sins[7] and strengthens us in the face of temptations. It is itself the bread of life that we need daily to grow into eternal life. It makes our will into an instrument at God's disposal. Thereby it lays the foundation for the kingdom of God in us and gives us clean lips and a pure heart to glorify God's holy name.

So we see again how the offertory, communion, and praise of God [in the Divine Office] are internally related. Participation in the sacrifice and in the sacrificial meal actually transforms the soul into a living stone in the city of God—in fact, each individual soul into a temple of God.

## 2. Solitary Dialogue with God as the Prayer of the Church

The individual human soul a temple of God—this opens to us an entirely new, broad vista. The prayer life of Jesus was to be the key to understanding the prayer of the church. We saw that Christ took part in the public and prescribed worship services of his people, i.e., in what one usually calls "liturgy." He brought the liturgy into the most intimate relationship with his sacrificial offering and so for the first time gave it its full and true meaning—that of thankful homage of creation to its Creator. This is precisely how he transformed the liturgy of the Old Covenant into that of the New.

But Jesus did not merely participate in public and prescribed worship services. Perhaps even more often the Gospels tell of solitary prayer in the still of the night, on open mountain tops, in the wilderness far from people. Jesus' public ministry was preceded by forty days and forty nights of prayer.[8] Before he chose and commissioned his twelve apostles, he withdrew into the isolation of the mountains.[9] By his hour on the Mount of Olives, he prepared himself for his road to Golgotha. A few short words tell us what he implored of his Father during this most difficult hour of his life, words that are given to us as guiding stars for our own hours on the Mount of Olives. "Father, if you are willing, take this cup away from me. Nevertheless, let your will be done, not mine."[10] Like lightning, these words for an instant illumine for us the innermost spiritual life of Jesus, the unfathomable mystery of his God-man existence and his dialogue with the Father. Surely, this dialogue was life-long and uninterrupted. Christ prayed interiorly not only when he had withdrawn from the crowd, but also when he was among people. And once he allowed us to look extensively and deeply at this secret dialogue. It was not long before the hour of the Mount of Olives; in fact, it was immediately before they set out to go there at the end of the Last Supper, which we recognize as the actual hour of the birth of the church. "Having loved his own..., he loved them to the end."[11] He knew that this was their last time together, and he wanted to give them as much as he in any way could. He had to restrain himself from saying more. But he surely knew that they could not bear any more, in fact, that they could not even grasp this little bit. The Spirit of Truth had to come first to open their eyes for it. And after he had said and done everything that he could say and do, he lifted his eyes to heaven and spoke to the Father in their presence.[12] We call these words Jesus' great high priestly prayer, for this talking alone with God also had its antecedent in the Old Covenant. Once a year on the greatest and most holy day of the year, on the Day of Atonement, the high priest stepped into the Holy of Holies before the face of the Lord "to pray for himself and his household and the whole congregation of Israel."[13] He sprinkled the throne of grace with the blood of a young bull and a goat, which he previously had to slaughter, and in this way absolved himself and his house "of the impurities of the sons of Israel and of their transgressions and of all their sins."[14] No person was to be in the tent (i.e., in the holy place that lay in front of the Holy of Holies) when the high priest stepped into God's presence in this awesomely sacred place, this place where no one but he entered and he himself only at this hour. And even now he had to burn incense "so that a cloud of smoke…would veil the judgment throne…and he not die."[15] This solitary dialogue took place in deepest mystery.

The Day of Atonement is the Old Testament antecedent of Good Friday. The ram that is slaughtered for the sins of the people represents the spotless Lamb of God (so did, no doubt, that other—chosen by lot and burdened with the sins of the people—that was driven into the wilderness). And the high priest descended from Aaron foreshadows the eternal high priest. Just as Christ anticipated his sacrificial death during the last supper, so he also anticipated the high priestly prayer. He did not have to bring for himself an offering for sin because he was without sin. He did not have to await the hour prescribed by the Law, nor to seek out the Holy of Holies in the temple. He stands, always and everywhere, before the face of God; his own soul is the Holy of Holies. It is not only God's dwelling, but is also essentially and indissolubly united to God. He does not have to conceal himself from God by a protective cloud of incense. He gazes upon the uncovered face of the Eternal One and has nothing to fear. Looking at the Father will not kill him. And he unlocks the mystery of the high priest's realm. All who belong to him may hear how, in the Holy of Holies of his heart, he speaks to his Father; they are to experience what is going on and are to learn to speak to the Father in their own hearts.[16]

The Savior's high priestly prayer unveils the mystery of the inner life: the circumincession of the Divine Persons and the indwelling of God in the soul. In these mysterious depths the work of salvation was prepared and accomplished itself in concealment and silence. And so it will continue until the union of all is actually accomplished at the end of time. The decision for the Redemption was conceived in the eternal silence of the inner divine life. The power of the Holy Spirit came over the Virgin praying alone in the hidden, silent room in Nazareth and brought about the Incarnation of the Savior. Congregated around the silently praying Virgin, the emergent church awaited the promised new outpouring of the Spirit that was to quicken it into inner clarity and fruitful outer effectiveness. In the night of blindness that God laid over his eyes, Saul awaited in solitary prayer the Lord's answer to his question, "What do you want me to do?"[17] In solitary prayer Peter was prepared for his mission to the Gentiles.[18] And so it has remained all through the centuries. In the silent dialogue with their Lord of souls consecrated to God, the events of church history are prepared that, visible far and wide, renew the face of the earth. The Virgin, who kept every word sent from God in her heart, is the model for such attentive souls in whom Jesus' high priestly prayer comes to life again and again. And women who, like her, were totally self-forgetful because they were steeped in the life and suffering of Christ, were the Lord's preferred choice as instruments to accomplish great things in the church: a St. Bridget, a Catherine of Siena. And when St. Teresa, the powerful reformer of her Order at a time of widespread falling away from the faith, wished to come to the rescue of the church, she saw the renewal of true interior life as the means toward this end. Teresa was very disturbed by the news of the continually spreading movement of apostasy:

> ...As though I could do something or were something, I cried to the Lord and begged him that I might remedy so much evil. It seemed to me that I would have given a thousand lives to save one soul out of the many that were being lost there. I realized I was a woman and wretched and incapable of doing any of the useful things I desired to do in the service of the Lord. All my longing was and still is that since He has so many enemies and so few friends that these few friends be good ones. As a result I resolved to do the little that was in my power; that is, to follow the evangelical counsels as perfectly as I could and strive that these few persons who live here do the same. I did this trusting in the great goodness of God.... Since we would all be occupied in continual prayer for those who are the defenders of the Church and for preachers and for learned men who protect her from attack, we could help as much as possible this Lord of mine who is so roughly treated by those for whom He has done so much good; it seems these traitors would want Him to be crucified again....
>
> O my Sisters in Christ, help me beg these things of the Lord. This is why he has gathered you together here. This is your vocation.[19]

To Teresa it seemed necessary to use:

> ...the approach of a lord when in time of war his land is overrun with enemies and he finds himself restricted on all sides. He withdraws to a city that he has well fortified and from there sometimes strikes his foe. Those who are in the city, being chosen people, are such that they can do more by themselves than many cowardly soldiers can. And often victory is won in this way....

But why have I said this? So that you understand, my Sisters, that what we must ask God is that in this little castle where there are already good Christians not one of us will go over to the enemy and that God will make the captains this castle..., who are the preachers and theologians, very advanced in the way of the Lord. Since most of them belong to religious orders, ask God that they advance very far in the perfection of religious life and their vocation....

These persons must live among men, deal with men..., and even sometimes outwardly behave as such men do. Do you think, my daughters, that little is required for them to deal with the world, live in the world, engage in its business..., while interiorly remaining its strangers...; in sum, not being men but angels? For if they do not live in this way, they do not deserve to be called captains; nor may the Lord allow them to leave their cells, for they will do more harm than good. This is not the time for seeing imperfections in those who must teach....

Is it not the world they have to deal with? Have no fear that the world will forgive this deficiency; nor is there any imperfection it fails to recognize. It will overlook many good things and perhaps not even consider them good; but have no fear that it will overlook any evil or imperfect things. Now I wonder who it is that teaches people in the world about perfection, not so much that these people might seek perfection..., but that they might condemn others.... So, then, do not think that little help from God is necessary for this great battle these preachers and theologians are fighting; a very great deal is necessary....

So, then, I beg you for the love of the Lord to ask His Majesty to hear us in this matter. Miserable though I am, I ask His Majesty this since it is for His glory and the good of the Church; this glory and good is the object of my desires....

And when your prayers, desires, disciplines, and fasts are not directed toward obtaining these things I mentioned, reflect on how you are not accomplishing or fulfilling the purpose for which the Lord brought you here together."[20]

What gave this religious, who had been living prayerfully in a monastery cell for decades, the passionate desire to do something for the church and the keen eye for the needs and demands of her time? It was precisely that she lived in prayer and allowed herself to be drawn ever more deeply by the Lord into the depths of her "interior castle" until she reached that obscure room where he could say to her, "that now it was time that she consider as her own what belonged to him, and that he would take care of what was hers."[21] Therefore, she could no longer do anything more than "with zeal be zealous for the Lord, the God of Hosts" (words of our Holy Father, Elijah, which have been taken as a motto on the shield of the Order). Whoever surrenders unconditionally to the Lord will be chosen by him as an instrument for building his kingdom. The Lord alone knows how much the prayer of St. Teresa and her daughters contributed to protect Spain from dissenting from the faith, and what power it exerted in the heated battles regarding the faith in France, the Netherlands, and Germany.

Official history is silent about these invisible and incalculable forces. But they are recognized by the trust of the faithful and the carefully balanced judgment of the church after extensive investigations. And our time is more and more determined, when all else fails, to hope for ultimate salvation from these hidden sources.

### 3. Inner Life and Outer Form and Action

The work of salvation takes place in obscurity and stillness. In the heart's quiet dialogue with God the living building blocks out of which the kingdom of God grows are prepared, the chosen instruments for the construction forged. The mystical stream that flows through all centuries is no spurious tributary that has strayed from the prayer life of the church—it is its deepest life. When this mystical stream breaks through traditional forms, it does so because the Spirit that blows where it will is living in it, this Spirit that has created all traditional forms and must ever create new ones. Without him there would be no liturgy and no church. Was not the soul of the royal psalmist a harp whose strings resounded under the gentle breath of the Holy Spirit? From the overflowing heart of the Virgin Mary blessed by God streamed the exultant hymn of the "Magnificat." When the angel's mysterious word became visible reality, the prophetic "Benedictus" hymn unsealed the lips of the old priest Zechariah, who had been struck dumb. Whatever arose from spirit-filled hearts found expression in words and melodies and continues to be communicated from mouth to mouth. The "Divine Office" is to see that it continues to resound from generation to generation. So the mystical stream forms the many-voiced, continually swelling hymn of praise to the triune God, the Creator, the Redeemer, and the Perfecter. Therefore, it is not a question of placing the inner prayer free of all traditional forms as "subjective" piety in contrast to the liturgy as the "objective" prayer of the church. All authentic prayer is prayer of the church. Through every sincere prayer something happens in the church, and it is the church itself that is praying therein, for it is the Holy Spirit living in the church that intercedes for every individual soul "with sighs too deep for words."[22] This is exactly what "authentic" prayer is, for "no one can say 'Jesus is Lord' except by the Holy Spirit."[23] What could the prayer of the church be, if not great lovers giving themselves to God who is love!

The unbounded loving surrender to God and God's return gift, full and enduring union, this is the highest elevation of the heart attainable, the highest level of prayer. Souls who have attained it are truly the heart of the church, and in them lives Jesus' high priestly love. Hidden with Christ in God, they can do nothing but radiate to other hearts the divine love that fills them and so participate in the perfection of all into unity in God, which was and is Jesus' great desire. This was how Marie Antoinette de Geuser understood her vocation. She had to undertake this highest Christian duty in the midst of the world. Her way is certainly a very meaningful and strengthening model for the many people who, having become radically serious about their inner lives, want to stand up for the church and who cannot follow this call into the seclusion of a monastery. The soul that has achieved the highest level of mystical prayer and entered into the "calm activity of divine life" no longer thinks of anything but of giving itself to the apostolate to which God has called it.

> This is repose in orderliness and, at the same time, activity free of all constraint. The soul conducts the battle in peace, because it is acting entirely from the viewpoint of eternal decrees. She knows that the will of her God will be perfectly fulfilled to his greater glory, because—though the human will often, as it were, sets limits for divine omnipotence—that divine omnipotence triumphs after all by creating something magnificent out of whatever material is left. This victory of divine power over human freedom, which he nevertheless permits to do as it pleases, is one of the most wonderful and adorable aspects of God's plan for the world....[24]

When Marie Antoinette de Geuser wrote this letter, she was near the threshold of eternity. Only a thin veil still separated her from that final consummation that we call living in glory.

For those blessed souls who have entered into the unity of life in God, everything is one: rest and activity, looking and acting, silence and speaking, listening and communicating, surrender in loving acceptance and an outpouring of love in grateful songs of praise. As long as we are still on the way—and the farther away from the goal the more intensely—we are still subject to temporal laws, and are instructed to actualize in ourselves, one after another and all the members complementing each other mutually, the divine life in all its fullness. We need hours for listening silently and allowing the Word of God to act on us until it moves us to bear fruit in an offering of praise and an offering of action. We need to have traditional forms and to participate in public and prescribed worship services so our interior life will remain vital and on the right track, and so it will find appropriate expression. There must be special places on earth for the solemn praise of God, places where this praise is formed into the greatest perfection of which humankind is capable. From such places it can ascend to heaven *for* the whole church and have an influence *on* the church's members; it can awaken the interior life in them and make them zealous for external unanimity. But it must be enlivened from within by this means: that here, too, room must be made for silent recollection. Otherwise, it will degenerate into a rigid and lifeless lip service.[25] And protection from such dangers is provided by those homes for the interior life where souls stand before the face of God in solitude and silence in order to be quickening love in the heart of the church.[26]

However, the way to the interior life as well as to the choirs of blessed spirits who sing the eternal *Sanctus* is Christ. His blood is the curtain through which we enter into the Holiest of Holies, the Divine Life. In baptism and in the sacrament of reconciliation, his blood cleanses us of our sins, opens our eyes to eternal light, our ears to hearing God's word. It opens our lips to sing his praise, to pray in expiation, in petition, in thanksgiving, all of which are but varying forms of adoration, i.e., of the creature's homage to the Almighty and All-benevolent One. In the sacrament of confirmation, Christ's blood marks and strengthens the soldiers of Christ so that they candidly profess their allegiance. However, above all, we are made members of the Body of Christ by virtue of the sacrament in which Christ himself is present. When we partake of the sacrifice and receive Holy Communion and are nourished by the flesh and blood of Jesus, we ourselves become his flesh and his blood. And only if and insofar as we are members of his Body, can his spirit quicken and govern us. "It is the Spirit that quickens, for the Spirit gives life to the members. But it only quickens members of its own body.... The Christian must fear nothing as much as being separated from the Body of Christ. For when separated from Christ's Body, the Christian is no longer his member, is no longer quickened by his Spirit...."[27] However, we become members of the Body of Christ "not only through love..., but in all reality, through becoming one with his flesh: For this is effected through the food that he has given us in order to show us his longing for us. This is why he has submerged himself in us and allowed his body to take form in us. We, then, are one, just as the body is joined to the head....."[28] As members of his Body, animated by his Spirit, we bring ourselves "through him, with him, and in him" as a sacrifice and join in the eternal hymn of thanksgiving. Therefore, after receiving the holy meal, the church permits us to say: "Satisfied by such great gifts, grant, we beseech you, Lord, that these gifts we have received be for our salvation and that we never cease praising you."[29]

# II
# *On God's Mercy*

## II.1. The Spirit of St. Elizabeth As It Informed Her Life

Why has our time developed such a fondness—we might even call it a craze—for jubilees? Could it be the oppressive burden of misery that arouses the desire to withdraw again and again for a short breathing spell from the gray, oppressive atmosphere of the present time and to warm oneself a little in the sun of better days? But such flight from the present would be an unproductive way to celebrate jubilees, and we may assume that a deeper, healthier desire, even if not clearly conscious of itself, motivates these glimpses into the past. A generation poor in spirit and thirsting for the spirit looks anywhere that it once flowed abundantly in order to drink of it. And that is a healing impulse. For the spirit is living and does not die. Wherever it was once at work in forming human lives and human structures, it leaves behind not only dead monuments, but leads therein a mysterious existence, like hidden and carefully tended embers that flare up brightly, glow and ignite as soon as a living breath blows on them. The lovingly penetrating gaze of the researcher who traces out the hidden sparks from the monuments of the past—this is the living breath that lets the flame flare up. Receptive human souls are the stuff in which it ignites and becomes the informing strength that helps in mastering and shaping present life. And if it was a holy fire that once burned here on the earth and left behind the traces of its action, then all the places and remains of this action are under holy protection. From the original source of all fire and light, the hidden embers are mysteriously nourished and preserved in order to break out again and again as an inexhaustible, productive source of blessing.

Such a source of blessing is revealed to us in the remembrance of the lovely saint who 700 years ago closed her eyes to this world as someone perfected early in order to enter into the radiant glory of eternal life. Her life story seems like a wondrous fairy tale. It is the story of the

19

Hungarian royal child, Elizabeth, who was born in the castle in Pressburg at the same time as the magician Klingsor in Eisenach read of her birth in the stars, and predicted her future fame and meaning for the Thuringia region.[1] The treasures that Queen Gertrud saved up to bestow in splendor on her little daughter sound like something out of *A Thousand and One Nights* and so also does the vehicle on which all of the splendors were loaded when Count Hermann of Thuringia sent for the four-year-old princess to be fetched to the far-away Wartburg as the bride for his son. The queen even promised to send a large dowry along later. But her relentless striving for riches, glitter, and power came to a sudden end. She was murdered by conspirators, and the child she had sent abroad to secure a crown became a motherless orphan.

The story of the children Ludwig and Elizabeth reminds us of the intimate relationships in German folk tales. They grew up together, loving each other deeply like brother and sister, and clung to each other in steadfast faithfulness when everything was working to separate them from one another, when everyone gradually turned away from the foreign and unusual child who would rather spend time with ragged beggars than celebrate joyful festivals, who seemed to fit better in a convent than on a royal throne as the center of a luxuriant, radiant life at court, to which the nobility of Thuringia had been accustomed on the Wartburg from the time of Count Hermann.

Then there follows a romance of chivalry, the young count's initiation into knighthood and the beginning of his reign, the glittering wedding and the young wedded bliss of the royal pair, Elizabeth's life as a countess at the side of her husband: festivals, hunts, horseback rides in all directions throughout their land. And placed amid all this was her silent concern for the poor and sick in the vicinity of the Wartburg. Then there came the increasing seriousness of a ruler's concerns: her husband's sallies into battle, regency in his absence, struggles against the hunger and pestilence that were bringing down the people, and simultaneously against the opposition of her surroundings that would not permit her to address these needs with all her strength. Finally, there was the Count's crusader vow, the deep pain of farewell and separation, the collapse of the distraught widow when she got the news of her husband's death. A woman's fate like that of many—so it seems.

But what happened next is new and has no parallel. She who is sunk in grief raises herself like a *mulier fortis* [strong woman], as the liturgy of her feast extols her, and takes her fate into her hands. At night during a storm, she leaves the Wartburg where people will no longer permit her to live as her conscience dictates. She seeks refuge for herself and her children in Eisenach, and because she cannot find bearable accommodations, she accepts for the time being the hospitality of her maternal relatives. And even when a reconciliation with the brothers of her husband has come about and she is returned to the Wartburg in utmost honor and brotherly love, she cannot stand it there for long. She must walk the path laid out for her to the end, must leave the place on the heights in order to live among the poorest of the poor as one of them, must place her children into strangers' hands, in order to belong to the Lord alone and to serve him in his suffering members. Stripped of everything, she vows herself to the Lord who gave everything for his own. On Good Friday in the year 1229, she puts her hands on the stripped altar of the Franciscan Church in Marburg and dons the clothing of the Order. She had belonged to it for years already as a tertiary without being able to live by its spirit as her heart desired. Now she is the sister of the poor and serves them in the hospital that she built for them. But not for very long, for only two years later her strength is exhausted and the twenty-four-year-old is permitted to enter into the joy of the Lord.

Here is life whose outer facts are colorful and appealing enough to arouse fantasy, to awaken amazement and admiration. But that is not why we are concerned with it. We would like to pursue what lies behind the outer facts, to feel the beat of the heart that bore such a fate and did such things, to internalize the spirit that governed her. All the facts reported about Elizabeth reveal one thing, all the words we have from her: a burning heart that comprehends everything around her with earnest, tenderly adaptable, and faithful love. This is how she put her hand as a little child into the hand of the boy whom the political power struggles of her ambitious parents had given her for her life's companion, never again to release it. This is how she shared her entire life with the playmates of her early childhood until shortly before her death, when her severe director took them from her to dissolve the last tie of earthly love. This is how in her heart she carried the children she bore when still almost a child herself. And when she gave them up, it was certainly out of a maternal love that did not want them to share her own all-too-hard path, as well as a maternal sense of duty that would not let her take away by her own hands the destiny to which their natural circumstances in life entitled them. But she also gave them up because she felt such overwhelming love that they would have become a hindrance in the vocation to which God was calling her.

From earliest youth she opened her heart in warm, compassionate love for all who suffered and were oppressed. She was moved to feed the hungry and to tend the sick, but was never satisfied with warding off material need alone, always desiring to have cold hearts warm themselves at her own. The poor children in her hospital ran into her arms calling her mother, because they felt her real maternal love. All of this overflowing treasure came from the inexhaustible source of the Lord's love, for he had been close to her for as long as she could remember. When her father and mother sent her away, he went with her into the faraway, foreign country. From the time she knew that he dwelt in the town chapel, she was drawn to it from the midst of her childhood games. Here she is at home. When people reviled and derided her, it was here that she found comfort. No one was as faithful as he. Therefore, she had to be true to him as well and love him above everyone and everything. No human image was permitted to dislodge his image from her heart. This is why strong pangs of remorse overwhelmed her when she was startled by the little bell announcing the consecration, making her aware that her eye and her heart were turned toward the husband at her side instead of paying attention to the Holy Sacrifice. In the presence of the image of the Crucified One who hangs on the Cross naked and bleeding, she could not wear finery and a crown. He stretched his arms out wide to draw to himself all who were burdened and heavy laden. She must carry this Crucified One's love to all who are burdened and heavy laden and in turn arouse in them love for the Crucified One. They are all members of the Mystical Body of Christ. She serves the Lord when she serves them. But she must also ensure that through faith and love they become living members. Everyone close to her she tried to lead to the Lord, thus practicing a blessed apostolate. This is evident in the life of her companions. The formation of her husband is a persuasive witness to this, as well as the interior change of his brother Conrad, who after her death, obviously under her influence, entered an Order. The love of Christ, this is the spirit that filled and informed Elizabeth's life, that nurtured her unceasing love of her neighbors.

We can comprehend Elizabeth's characteristic contagious happiness as arising from the same source. She loved turbulent children's games and continued to take pleasure in them long after, in accordance with the usual ideas of breeding and custom, she was supposed to have outgrown them. She enjoyed everything beautiful. She dressed very well and put on splendid parties that delighted her guests, as was her duty in her position as a countess. Above all, she wanted to bring joy to the huts of the poor. She took toys to the children and played with them herself. Even the sullen widow whom she had for a housemate during the last part of her life could not dim her enthusiasm and had to be pleased by her jokes. And she was moved by the poor to the depths of her heart on that day when she invited them to Marburg by the thousands and singlehandedly distributed among them the remainder of the widow's pension that had been given to her in cash. From morning to evening she walked through the rows giving each one a share. As night came on, many remained who were too weak and sick to make their way home. They encamped in the open, and Elizabeth had fires lit for them. This made them feel good, and songs arose around the campfires. Amazed, the countess listened, and it confirmed for her what she had believed and practiced all her life: "See, I told you that all one has to do is to make the poor happy." That God had created his creatures for happiness had long been her conviction, and she felt it was proper to lift a radiant face to him. And this was also confirmed for her at her death when she was called to eternal joy by the sweet song of a little bird.

Overflowing love and joy led to a free naturalness that could not be contained by convention. How could one walk in measured stride or lisp pretentious speech when the signal resounds before the castle gate, announcing the master's return? Elizabeth forgot irretrievably all the rules of breeding when her heart began beating stormily, and she followed the rhythm and beat of her heart. Again, is one to think about socially acceptable forms for expressing one's devotion even in church? She could only do what love asked of her, even though it produced strong criticism. In no way could she understand that it was improper to take gifts to the poor herself, to speak with them in a friendly way, to go into their huts, and to care for them in their own homes. She did not want to be stubborn and disobedient and to live in discord with her own, but she could not hear human voices over the inner voice governing her. Therefore, in the long run she could not live among the conventional, who could not and would not release themselves from age-old institutions and deeply rooted ways of thinking about life. She was able to remain among her peers as long as a holy union held her fast and a faithful protector remained at her side, sympathetically taking into consideration her heart's command while at the same time prudently considering the demands of the surroundings. After the death of her husband, she had to leave the circles into which she was born and raised and to go her own way. It was a sharp and painful separation, certainly for her as well. But with a heart full of love that was stopped by no barriers separating her from her dear brothers and sisters, she found the path that so many today vainly seek, despite their great good will and the exertion of all their strength: the path to the hearts of the poor.

All through the centuries there runs a human longing that is never put to rest. Sometimes it is expressed softly, at other times more loudly. One who felt it particularly poignantly found a catchy phrase for it: return to nature. And someone who with a consuming longing vainly pursued this ideal his entire life, until he collapsed, has drawn an unusually impressive picture of the person whose every action springs from the depths in a continual motion without reflection or exertion of the will, guided by the command of the heart alone: "One would have the charm of a marionette."[2]

Does St. Elizabeth conform to this ideal? The facts presented so far, pointing to her spontaneous way of doing things, seem to say so. But the sources recount other facts that no less clearly point to a will as hard as steel, to a relentless battle against her own nature: The lovely, youthfully cheerful, enchantingly natural person is at the same time a strictly ascetic saint. Early enough she had to recognize that giving oneself over to the pull of one's heart without restraint is not without its dangers. Extravagant love of her relatives, pride, and greed caused Queen Gertrud to be hated by the Hungarian people, caused her sudden, unexpected death at the hands of murderers. Untamed passion led Gertrud's sister, Agnes of Meran, into a relationship with the king of France that broke up his marriage and brought ecclesiastical censure to all of France. Reckless political ambition entangled Count Hermann in a lifetime of unremitting warfare and left him to die while excommunicated. From time to time Elizabeth even had to see her own husband involved in unjust power struggles and anathematized. And was even she free of these sinister forces in her own breast? By no means! She knew very well that she, too, could not give herself over to the guidance of her own heart without danger.

When, with cunning piety, the child thought up games that would allow her to skip off to the chapel or throw herself down secretly to say her prayers, a mighty tug of grace must certainly have been working in her heart; but she could have suspected, too, that in her play she was also in danger of getting lost from God. This becomes even clearer when the young lady came home from her first dance with a serious face and said, "One dance is enough for the world. For God's sake, I want to forego the rest of them." When she arose from her bed at night and knelt to pray or left the room entirely to let the maids whip her, this surely tells us not only of her general desire to do penance and to suffer voluntarily for the Lord's sake, but that she wanted to save herself from the danger of forgetting the Lord while at her beloved husband's side. Surely Elizabeth's natural sense of beauty was drawn to pretty children rather than to ugly ones, and was repelled by the appearance and odor of disgusting wounds. Therefore, since she repeatedly sought out such ailing creatures to tend to them herself, this tells not only of her compassionate love for the poorest, but also of the will to overcome her natural revulsion. Even during the last years of her life Elizabeth prayed to God for three things: for contempt for all earthly goods, for the gift of cheerfully bearing humiliation, and to be free of excessive love for her children. She could tell her maids that she was heard in all of this. But that she had to ask for these things showed they were not natural for her, and that she had probably been struggling for them in vain for a long time.

Forming her life to please God—Elizabeth strives for this goal not only for herself and in battle against her own nature. With full awareness and the same inflexible determination, she endeavors to influence her surroundings. As countess she takes pains to counteract excesses in sumptuous clothing and to move the titled ladies to renounce this or that vanity. When she begins to avoid all food obtained with illegal revenues and is thus often forced to go hungry at the fully laden royal table, she assumes that her loyal companions Guda and Isentrud will share her deprivations, as later they will also follow her into the distress of voluntary banishment and poverty. And what a protest this abstention from food was against the whole way of life around her!

Her increasingly austere way of life made most severe demands on her husband. He had to look on while she treated herself with the utmost harshness, endangered her health, squandered his wealth lavishly; while, by all this, she roused the opposition of his family and of all at court; and, finally, while she fought to detach herself interiorly from him, even bemoaning bitterly that she was bound by her marriage. All this required heroic self-mastery on his part as well, and one readily understands why, as he accepted everything with love and patience, faithfully taking the trouble to stand by his wife in her striving for perfection, the young count came to be regarded as a saint by his people.

Initially, it was probably the doctrine of the Gospel and the general ascetic practices of her time that guided Elizabeth in her striving for perfection. Every now and then she had an insight and sought to put it into practice. When the Franciscans came to Germany, she found what she was looking for, a clearly outlined ideal and complete way of life; and, as her guest on the Wartburg, Rodiger instructed her about the lifestyle of the Poor Man of Assisi. Now suddenly she knew precisely what she wanted and what she had always longed for: to be entirely poor, to go begging from door to door, to be no longer chained by any possessions or human ties, also to be free of her own will—to be entirely and exclusively the Lord's own. Count Ludwig could not bring himself to dissolve the marriage bond, to let her leave him. However, he would help her toward a regulated life, approximating her ideal as closely as possible. It was probably better for her guide not to be a Franciscan—otherwise her unfulfillable wishes could not be put to rest—but someone who dampened her excesses with quiet reason and yet had an understanding of her interior desire. Such a man was Master Conrad of Marburg who was recommended to the count as a guide for his wife. He was a secular priest but as poor as a beggar monk, entirely consecrated to the service of the Lord, and very strict with himself as well as with others. This is how he traveled throughout Germany as preacher of the crusade and warrior for the purity of the faith. Elizabeth took a vow to obey him in the year 1225 and remained under his direction until her death. For her to submit herself to him and to continue submissive to him was surely the most severe breaking of her own will, for, in accordance with her own wishes, he not only engaged in the severest battle against her lower nature, but also directed her love of God and neighbor in directions different from her impulse. Neither before nor after the death of her husband did he ever permit her to give up all her possessions. He restrained her indiscriminate almsgiving, gradually limited it and finally completely forbade it to her. He also tried to keep her from tending people with contagious diseases (the only point on which Elizabeth had not entirely submitted by the end).

Certainly his ideal of perfection was not inferior to hers. It was clear to him from the beginning that he was entrusted with the guidance of a saintly soul, and he wanted to do everything he could to lead her to the summit of perfection. But his opinions about the means thereto differed from hers. In the first place, he wanted to teach her to strive for the ideal *where she was,* just as he had not considered it necessary to enter an Order himself. So he permitted her to join the Franciscans as a tertiary and interpreted the vows for her in a way appropriate to her state in life. As long as her husband was living she was to perform all her marital duties, but to renounce remarriage if he died. She was to live a life of poverty but not carelessly squander what she had, rather providing sensibly for the poor. Foremost in this life of poverty was the food ban that prohibited her all nourishment not obtained from lawful revenues. Carrying out this prohibition (according to recent research) is said to be what caused her to leave the Wartburg after the death of her husband. It is assumed that her brother-in-law, Heinrich Raspe, was unwilling to tolerate her absenting herself from the royal table, and cut off her widow's pension to coerce her (surely also to put an end to her wasteful good deeds). After the extreme need and abandonment that she suffered from this voluntary or involuntary banishment, she could not bear to become reaccustomed to her former circumstances. She only returned to the Wartburg temporarily after her reconciliation with the count's family and immediately began to discuss with Master Conrad the best way of realizing her Franciscan ideal. He agreed to none of her suggestions, allowing neither entrance into a convent nor the assumption of a hermit or beggar life. He could not prevent her from renewing her vows or from allowing herself to be clothed in the dress of the Order. And he let her take up residence in her city of Marburg where he lived, too. He determined a lifestyle for her in accord with his judgment, by using her means to build a hospital in Marburg and assigning her certain duties in it. It was probably her own idea not to use any of her income for herself, but to earn her subsistence by her own hands (by spinning wool for the Altenburg monastery), and her director agreed. In Master Conrad's opinion, the most difficult and important task was to teach his charge obedience. It was his pious conviction that obedience was better than sacrifice, that there was no way to attain perfection without letting go of all of one's own wishes and inclinations. And his enthusiasm for his goal drew him into corporal punishment when she repeatedly overstepped his orders. Certainly, deep within Elizabeth agreed with him. This is evident not only by the patience and meekness with which she bore these severe humiliations. She would certainly not have conceded on such an essential point as the renunciation of her greatly desired lifestyle if she had not been convinced of the importance of obedience. She saw God's representative in the director given to her, whom she had not chosen herself. More unerringly than the tug of her own heart, his word disclosed God's will. In the last analysis, it finally comes down to one thing: forming one's life according to God's will. Thus, they both wage a relentless struggle against natural inclinations.

Sometimes it is Elizabeth herself who takes the lead and finds only the master's approval, as in the move to Marburg and the separation from her children. Sometimes Conrad commands and Elizabeth submits obediently to him, such as when he takes away the beloved companions of her youth and substitutes housemates that are hard to bear, when he increasingly restricts her joy of personally giving alms and finally entirely prohibits it. There was only *one* point on which she would not totally concede. Along with her service at the hospital, she insisted on continuing to have with her a child sick with a particularly unbearable illness in her own little house next door and to care for the child all alone. A little fellow ill with scabies even sat beside her death bed, as Master Conrad himself told Pope Gregory IX, who had entrusted to him the care of the widow after the death of the count. Immediately after her death, Master Conrad enthusiastically urged Pope Gregory to beatify her.

So we seem to get a conflicting picture of the saint and the formation of her life. On the one hand we have a stormy temperament that spontaneously follows the instincts of a warm, love-filled heart uninhibited by her own reflection or outside objections. On the other hand we see a forcefully grasping will constantly trying to subdue its own nature and compelling her life to conform to an externally prescribed pattern on the basis of rigid principles that consciously contradicted the inclinations of her heart.

However, there is a standpoint from which the contradictions can be understood and finally harmoniously resolved, that alone truly fulfills this longing to be natural. Those who avow an "unspoiled human nature" assume that people possess a molding power operating from the inside undisturbed by the push and pull of external influence, shaping people and their lives into harmonious, fully formed creatures. But experience does not substantiate this lovely belief. The form is indeed hidden within, but trapped in many webs that prevent its pure realization. People who abandon themselves to their nature soon find themselves driven to and fro by it and do not arrive at a clear formation or organization. And formlessness is not naturalness. Now people who take control of their own nature, curtailing rampant impulses, and seeking to give them the form that appears good to them, perhaps a ready made

form from outside, can possibly now and again give the inner form room
to develop freely. But it can also happen that they do violence to the
inner form and that, instead of a nature freely unfolded, the unnatural
and artificial appears.

Our knowledge is piecemeal. When our will and action build on it
alone, they cannot achieve a perfect structure. Nor can that knowledge,
because it does not have complete power over the self and often col-
lapses before reaching the goal. And so this inner shaping power that is
in bondage strains toward a light that will guide more surely, and a
power that will free it and give it space. This is the light and the power of
divine grace. Mighty was the tug of grace in the soul of the child Elizabeth. It set her on fire, and the flame of the love of God flared up, breaking through every cloak and barrier. Then this human child placed
herself in the hands of the divine Creator. Her will became pliant material for the divine will, and, guided by this will, it could set about taming
and curtailing her nature to channel the inner form. Her will could also
find an outer form suitable to its inner one and a form into which she
could grow without losing her natural direction. And so she rose to that
perfected humanity, the pure consequence of a nature freed and clari-
fied by the power of grace. On these heights it is safe to follow the impulses of one's heart, because one's own heart is united with the divine
heart and beats with its pulse and rhythm. Here Augustine's astute saying can serve as the guideline for forming a life: *Ama et fac quod vis [Love
and do what you will]*.

Carmel of Cologne-Lindenthal, destroyed by Allied bombing in 1944. Edith entered here on October 15, 1933.

# II.2. Love for Love:
# The Life and Works of St. Teresa of Jesus

## Foreword

Yesterday in our monastery church we had perpetual adoration [forty hours devotion]. On such days, the faithful who are associated with our Carmel gather around the altar singing and praying from about six o'clock in the morning until about ten o'clock at night. Then the church is closed and during the night the sisters take turns keeping watch in the choir before the Blessed Sacrament. While outside in carnival's frantic tumult people get drunk and delirious, while political battles separate them, and great need depresses them so much that many forget to look to heaven, at such still places of prayer hearts are opened to the Lord. In place of the cold, the contempt, that he receives out there, they offer him their warm love. They want to atone for the insults that the divine heart must endure daily and hourly. By their steadfast supplications, they draw down God's grace and mercy on a humanity submerged in sin and need. In our time, when the powerlessness of all natural means for battling the overwhelming misery everywhere has been demonstrated so obviously, an entirely new understanding of the power of prayer, of expiation, and of vicarious atonement has again awakened. This is why people of faith crowd the places of prayer, also why, everywhere, there is a blazing demand for contemplative monasteries whose entire life is devoted to prayer and expiation. Also suddenly there is talk in all corners and parts about the silent Carmel that just a few years ago was a little known country. The desire for new foundations is surfacing in the most varied places. One almost feels transported into the time when our Holy Mother Teresa, the foundress of the reformed Carmel, traveled all over Spain from north to south and from west to east to plant new vineyards of the Lord. One would like to bring into our times also something of the spirit of this great woman who built amazingly during a century of battles and disturbances. May she herself bless this little picture of her life and works, that it may capture at least some of the radiance of her spirit and convey it to the hearts of readers. Then surely will people desire to know her better from the sources, from the rich treasure of her own works. And whoever has learned to draw from these sources will never tire of gaining courage and strength from them again and again.

*Carmel of Cologne-Lindenthal, Candlemas [February 2], 1934.*

## 1. Native Land and Family Home

As a contemporary, spiritual relative, and native of the same country as that famous champion of the faith, St. Ignatius of Loyola, Teresa's impact unfolded in a century marked by religious strife and a great schism in the church. When she came into the world, a mere twenty years had passed since the last of the Moors were driven out of Spain and the whole peninsula united in the Catholic faith. Eight centuries of continual warfare between the Cross and the Crescent lay behind the Spanish people. During these battles they blossomed into an heroic people, into a legion of Christ the King. Teresa's more immediate homeland, the ancient kingdom of Castile, was the strong fortress from which in resolute struggle the cross was gradually carried to the South. The Castilian knights formed the special troops of the army of faith. Teresa, bold warrior for God, came from such a race of heroes. A town built on cliffs, the fortress of Avila (called "Avila of the Saints") was her native town. Her parents, Alonso Sánchez de Cepeda and his second wife Beatriz de Ahumada, were of the old nobility.[1] According to the custom of the times and of her country, she was called by her mother's surname, Teresa de Ahumada. Just as she saw the light of day on the morning of March 28, 1515, the bell of the newly built Carmelite monastery invited the faithful to a great celebration, to the consecration of its chapel.[2] This was the house that later was to be her home for decades, where the Lord intended to form this vessel of his election. Teresa was the sixth child of her father, the third of her young mother, who had taken charge of the daughter and two sons from her husband's first marriage. Six younger siblings were later added to these five older ones. Alonso Sánchez de Cepeda was a man of deep piety and strong virtue. He carefully watched over the upbringing of his children, sought to keep all harmful influences from them, guided them to everything good, and himself presented them with the best example of a serious Christian life. Delicate Doña Beatriz, mild and humble, ill at an early age , and dependent on the help of her stepdaughter María for the upbringing of this great band of children, was fervently devout. The love of God and of prayer bloomed spontaneously in the hearts of the children who shared her life.

## 2. Childhood and Youth

The fiery heart of the little Teresa became attached to her noble parents in ardent love and devotion and to her siblings in affectionate trust. Her most beloved companions had to be, primarily, her brothers. Serious María, burdened with the duties of the eldest, was not regarded as a comrade, and the baby, Juana, was many years younger. Rodrigo, four years older than she, became her confidant during her childhood. Her mother's pious tales, her first instruction, ignited in the little Spaniard a holy zeal. Despite her liveliness and joy in merry company, she liked to withdraw into a quiet corner of the garden to pray alone. It gave her pleasure to give alms to the poor. And one day the seven-year-old let her favorite brother in on a secret plan that she had thought up. She tells about it herself in her autobiography. "We were reading the lives of saints together. When I saw what torments the martyrs endured for God, I discovered that they had earned the joy of seeing God for a low price, and I burned with the desire to die a similar death" [L, 1, 1].[3] She did not have far to go from the wish to the decision to act, and her brother was also enkindled by her enthusiasm. "We decided to travel to the land of the Moors to get our heads cut off. It seemed to me that God had given us enough strength to carry out our plans in spite of our tender years. What was the most difficult for us was parting from our parents." But the thought of eternal joy won over the pain of separation. "Forever! Oh Rodrigo, think of it, the martyrs gaze upon God forever. We must become martyrs." The very next morning they secretly set out on their way. But they did not get far. They slipped through the town gate happily. But soon afterward they met an uncle who took the little fugitives back to their parents. They had already been missed and were greeted with reproach. "I left," Teresa replied, "because I want to see God and because one must die in order to see him." She was very hurt that her lovely plan had fallen apart. Her zeal did not abate. She built hermitages with Rodrigo in the garden, she preferred to play monastery life with her friends, and she continued her lengthy devotions.

The early death of her mother cut deeply into Teresa's youth. She was then thirteen years old.[4] She herself says about it, "I threw myself down in despair before an image of the Mother of God. With many tears, I implored the Holy Virgin to become my mother now. Uttered with the simplicity of a child, this prayer was heard. From that hour on, I never prayed to the Virgin in vain" [L, 1, 7]. The young person certainly surmised that she needed special protection, having lost her mother just when she especially needed her. Teresa had blossomed into a young beauty. Black curls framed her white forehead; luminous dark eyes revealed the passion of her soul; her movements and posture had natural grace and dignity. The liveliness of her spirit, her charming amiability, gave her an attractiveness in her social life that almost no one could resist. The dangers already inherent in these natural gifts were increased by an inclination that had already awakened in the young girl during her mother's life. Doña Beatriz, who was constantly house-bound by her suffering, liked to find a little distraction in romances of chivalry and was weak enough to allow her children to read them, too, even though this was not the father's intent. After her death, Teresa gave in to her passion without restraint and devoured one book after the other, busying herself with them day and night. Those novels are forgotten today, but we know their character from the magnificent satire, Cervantes' *Don Quixote,* which exposed for all time such writings and their impact. The "Knight of the Woeful Countenance" who mistook windmills for giants and a peasant girl for a princess, is the victim of such caricatures of real life. Teresa's active imagination was also enchanted by such entrancing portrayals of the deeds of heroic knights. The gentle attraction of the pious legends of her childhood paled against these colorful exploits. With bitter regret, she herself later looked back on these youthful mistakes.

> Oh, how I suffer now when I recall how I forgot the longings of my childhood! My God, since you seem to have decided to rescue me, let it be your glorious will to do so…. Why did this soul, which you have selected for your habitation and showered with grace, become spotted like this? I feel great pain remembering it, for I know very well that I alone was guilty. You, Oh Lord, have left nothing untried to open my eyes ever since my youngest days. [L, 1, 7-8]

It was not surprising that the young girl began to compare herself with the heroines of her beloved novels.

> There came a time when I understood the natural gifts that heaven had bestowed on me…. Soon I acquired a taste for beautiful clothes; I wanted to appear well-dressed; I took many pains with my hands and my hair; I resorted to every lovely scent and beauty aid that I could lay hands on. Above all, I loved meticulous cleanliness. I really did not have any ulterior motives at all in my heart, and for all the world I did not want anyone to get an idea of offending God. [L, 1, 8; 2, 2]

The young beauty did not lack admirers. However, her strict father would not permit her to associate with young strangers, but cousins of the same age were allowed in the house. "They liked me, and we spent time together. I let them talk as they would. I enlivened their conversation and, to please them, I took pleasure in their dreams of the future, in their childish misdeeds, and other useless things. However, the worst was that I learned about feelings and attitudes that were later to be unfortunate for me" [L, 2, 2]. The influence of one young relative was particularly unhealthy.

> She was so frivolous that my mother, as if guessing the bad results, tried everything to keep her away from me. But it was in vain. She always returned under this or that pretext. Soon we were close confidantes. We talked together constantly. She gave me as much pleas-

ure as I wanted, allowed me to share in hers, and confided her secrets and conceits to me. I couldn't get enough of listening to her. I believe I was a little over fourteen years old when our unhealthy friendship started. I believe that in this first period of my life I did not commit even one mortal sin. What saved me was the fear of God and, I must say, the even greater fear of staining my honor; for my honor was everything to me, and nothing in the world, no earthly good, could have shaken my decision to keep it pure. [L, 2, 3]

Nevertheless, the effect was deep enough. "This friendship changed me so much that soon there was nothing left of my good nature. My relative and one of her equally frivolous girl friends seemed to have imprinted the frivolity of their characters on me" [L, 2, 4]. Her father and older sister, who tended the younger siblings with motherly concern, saw the transformation with serious alarm and made a definite decision. When María left her family home to go to the house of a pious nobleman as his wife, Don Alonso sent his darling to an Augustinian monastery to be educated. Suddenly and without saying good-bye, she vanished from the merry circle of which she had been the center.

### 3. The Monastery Pupil

The monastery of Our Lady of Grace was highly regarded in Avila. The first families of the city entrusted it with their daughters. Teresa felt as if she were in prison during her first days behind the monastery walls, but soon the solitude aroused strong repentance for the past months. She was tormented by pangs of conscience. But this painful state of affairs did not last long. She again found her peace of mind and also quickly adjusted to boarding school life. With grateful love she attached herself to the boarding school directress, María Briceño, a devout nun and an outstanding educator.

Among the nuns I found one who was especially designated to supervise the pupils. Her bed was in our dormitory. It was she whom God designated to open my eyes. Her conversation seemed beneficial to me. She spoke so beautifully of God! I loved to listen to her. She told me how, upon reading the words of the Gospel, "Many are called but few are chosen," she made the decision to leave the world. She also reflected for me the joy that God reserves for those who leave everything for the love of him. While listening to her, I forgot the recent past. I felt the thought, the longing for eternal things awakening in me. My great aversion to monastic life more and more disappeared....

I only stayed in this monastery for one and one-half years, though I had made great progress in goodness there. I asked the nuns for their prayers that God would show me a way of life in which

I could best serve him. In my heart I was afraid that it could be a call to a monastery, just as I was afraid of marriage. Toward the end of my stay in the monastery, however, my inclinations turned more and more to the religious life. Since I believed that I was nevertheless not up to some of the practices of this monastery, I could not decide on this order. Moreover, I had a dear friend in a monastery of another convent. Uppermost in my mind was choosing a house where I could be with her. I was thinking less of the salvation of my soul than of the inclination of my nature. These good thoughts of becoming a nun arose now and then, but left again without my making a definite decision.... [L, 2, 10; 3, 1-2]

## 4. Vocational Decision

Still unclear about her future life's path, Teresa returned to her father's house. A serious illness occasioned her return. During her convalescence, she was sent to the farm of her sister María, who surrounded her with tender love and would have preferred to keep her permanently. But her father was unwilling to be deprived of her company any longer. He picked her up himself but left her en route with his brother Pedro Sánchez de Cepeda in Hortigosa for a few weeks, since he himself had to finish some pressing business.

Teresa's stay with her uncle was to be of decisive importance for her. His life was devoted entirely to prayer and to being occupied with spiritual books. He asked Teresa to read to him. "Actually," she writes, "this bored me a little. However, I gave the impression that I did so gladly anyhow, because I was overly compliant in order to give others pleasure" [L, 3, 4]. This time it was not to her detriment. Soon she was very much taken by the books her uncle gave her. The *Letters* of St. Jerome and St. Gregory's *Morals*, and the writings of St. Augustine captivated her active spirit and reawakened in her the pious enthusiasm of her childhood. The reading was often interrupted, and the pious old man and the young reader discussed the questions of eternal life in connection with it. Teresa's resolve ripened in this environment. She took a glance at her past life. What would have become of her if the Lord had called her from life during the time of vanity and infidelity? She does not want to expose herself to this danger again. From then on, eternal salvation is to be her goal, and, in order not to lose sight of it again, she will heroically conquer her aversion to religious life, her love of freedom, and her tender attachment to her father and siblings.

After the interior battle came a difficult outer one. In spite of all his piety, Don Alonso does not want to be separated from his favorite daughter. All her pleas, and the advocacy of her uncle and siblings, are in vain. But Teresa is no less decisive than her father. Since she cannot hope for his consent, she secretly leaves home. As in her earlier childish adventure, one of her brothers accompanies her. It is not Rodrigo, for he no longer lives at home, having taken a post in the Spanish colonies in America. Antonio, who is two years younger than Teresa, takes his place. She herself says:

> While I was settling on my leaving, I persuaded one of my brothers to leave the world by pointing out its frivolities to him. We agreed to set out early in the morning and that my brother himself would take me to the monastery.... But when I stepped over the threshold of my family home, such fear gripped me that I believed I could hardly be more afraid at the hour of my death. It was as if my bones were being separated from one another. The love for God was not strong enough in me to triumph over the love for my relatives. My natural feelings arose with such force that, in spite of all my deliberations, without God's support I would not have taken one more step. But God gave me courage in spite of myself and I set out. [L, 4, 1]

Antonio took his sister to the door of the Carmelite monastery. Then he himself went to the Dominican monastery of St. Thomas and asked for admission. This was on All Souls Day of the year 1535.

### 5.In the Monastery of the Incarnation: Novitiate

The house that in her childish reflections Teresa preferred over the Augustinians because a dear friend lived there (Juana Suárez, the blood sister of her teacher María Briceño) was the Carmelite Monastery of the Incarnation. It also had a number of other material advantages that could prejudice a receptive disposition: its magnificent location, its beautiful, spacious buildings, its expansive garden through which flowed clear streams. But these earthly motives were no longer decisive. "In spite of my preference for the monastery where my friend lived, I felt ready to enter some other one should I have had the hope of serving God better there or should it have been my father's wish. For I was seriously seeking the salvation of my soul and placed little value on quiet living" [L, 2, 2]. So it was clearly God's mysterious grace guiding her that gave her the inner certainty of where to direct her steps.

The *Order of the Most Blessed Virgin of Mount Carmel*, to which Teresa now belonged, already looked back on a long and glorious past. It revered as its founder the Prophet Elijah who led a hermit's life of prayer and fasting with his disciples in the caves of Mount Carmel. When his prayer freed the land of Israel from a drought that had lasted for years, then (according to the Order's legend) in a little cloud that signaled the saving rain, his prophetic vision recognized the image of the Virgin who would bear God, she who would bring grace. He is said to have been the first to revere the Mother of God, and the first shrine to Mary is said to have stood on the lovely heights of Mount Carmel. During the time of the crusades, the hermits of Mount Carmel were organized as an order. At their request, Patriarch Albert of Jerusalem gave them a Rule for their Order around 1200. In solitude and silence, they were to meditate on the law of the Lord day and night, to observe strict fasts as of old, and to obtain what they needed to live by the work of their own hands, as the apostle Paul exhorted. The persecution of religious by the Moslem conquerors of the Holy Land led to the transplantation of the Order to the West. Here the destiny of other orders at the beginning of the Middle Ages befell them also. The strict discipline of old gave way to a certain mitigation. Pope Eugene IV moderated the original Rule; and the first women's monasteries of the Order were founded in the fifteenth century on the basis of these moderated regulations. They also were observed at the Monastery of the Incarnation. It had only been in existence for a few decades before Teresa entered, and one could not accuse it of abuses. The existing regulations were being followed. Nuns of deep piety and of exemplary conduct lived there, but there was scarcely a trace left of the strong spirit of the original Carmel. The rich appointments of the monastery permitted a comfortable life; the old fasts and penances were for the most part abolished; there was great freedom of association with people in the world. The influx to this attractive place was so great that the monastery numbered 190 nuns in 1560. Still, the framework given it by its Constitutions continued to offer the full possibility of a true life of prayer. Teresa progressed through the school of the interior life to perfection here.

The last shadow to her happiness as a young novice vanished when Don Alonso subsequently gave his consent to her decision and, with a holy zeal, set about to challenge his young daughter in climbing the mountain of perfection, doing so in fact under her direction. She took up religious life with the same determination with which she had left her father's house, eagerly turned to prayer, the practices of obedience, and sisterly love. The reward was superabundant. If Teresa's resolute decision had been based mainly on the fear of God's judgment and on concern about her eternal salvation, these original motives soon receded in the face of God's love blazing up powerfully.

> At the same time as I put on the holy habit, God showed me his preference for those who constrain themselves in his service. I also felt so happy in my new position that this blessed feeling still continues. Nothing could rob me of this delight. God changed the dryness that could bring me to doubt into love for him.
>
> All the monastic practices were congenial to me. I often had to mop the floor in hours during which formerly I had dressed or amused myself. Just the thought of being free of all of these silly

things gave me renewed joy. I did not understand the source of so much joy.

As I think about it, there is no difficulty then that I would not have the courage to overcome. I know from experience that as soon as one has firmly decided right from the beginning to pursue one's goal for the honor of God without considering the opposition of one's nature, one is soon also rewarded. In order to increase our merits, God wants the soul to undergo an indescribable anxiety before one sets to work. But the greater this anxiety, the greater, later, is the delight. [L, 4, 2]

With holy joy the young novice participated in choral prayer. But the prescribed prayer times were not sufficient for her zeal. She also was happiest spending her free hours in silent contemplation before the tabernacle. It goes without saying that souls who did not like prayer as much accused her of exaggeration. But she let nothing stop her on her way. God's love gave her natural amiability and readiness to serve a new incentive and higher motivation when dealing with people. She felt that a day was lost if she did not do some work of charity. She welcomed the smallest opportunity for doing so. She took particular pleasure in caring for the sick. She enveloped with tender care a nun who was dying of a terrible disease that disgusted everyone else, and tried in every way to show that she was not at all repelled. This sick person's patience so strongly aroused her wonder that there was awakened in her a desire for similar trials.

...I asked God that, provided he were graciously to give me this patience, that he would also send me the most horrible diseases. I had the feeling of fearing none of them. I experienced such a strong desire for eternal goods that I would use any means to get them. Now I wonder at this myself, for at that time I did not yet have that love of God in me that I later found in meditative prayer. It was an inner light that let me recognize the little value of everything transitory and the immeasurable value of the eternal. [L, 5, 2]

Soon her pleas were to be heard.

## 6. The School of Suffering: Interior Life

Not long after her profession (November 3, 1537), heart problems sent her to the infirmary. She bore the pain, the forced idleness, the inability to participate in the religious practices, with no less patience than that of the nun who had amazed her. So she won the love of all the other sisters, even those who had formerly criticized and misinterpreted her actions. Her fond father wanted everything possible to be done and, because the doctors could not help, decided to take his daughter to a healer who was famous for her cures. Since the Monastery of the Incarnation was not enclosed, there was no hesitation about allowing her family to care for the young sister. The long trip took them first past Hortigosa. Pedro Sánchez gave Teresa a book [i.e., the *Third Spiritual Alphabet*] by Fr. [Francisco de] Osuna about the prayer of recollection, which was soon to become her guide. The travelers spent the winter at the farmhouse of María de Cepeda. Even though as in earlier years she was here surrounded by her loved ones, and devoted herself wholeheartedly to them, Teresa knew how to arrange the day to give herself enough time for solitary prayer; and so she remained faithful to her religious vocation outside the monastery setting. However, her illness steadily increased so that it was a relief when spring came, the time the healer of Becedas had designated for the cure. The long journey was a torment for the patient, but the cure was even worse. Instead of healing her, it only increased her suffering. In spite of all her agonizing pain, she steadfastly continued in contemplative prayer according to the directions in her spiritual guidebook, and God rewarded this courageous fidelity by even then raising her to a high level of the interior life.

In her writings, this doctor of prayer later presented the mystical life of grace in all its stages with incomparable clarity.[5] The neophyte who was beginning to practice prayer did not yet know what was happening in her soul. But in order to make her further development intelligible, it is necessary to say a few words here about the interior life.

Prayer is the communication of the soul with God. God is love, and love is goodness giving itself away. It is a fullness of being that does not want to remain enclosed in itself, but rather to share itself with others, to give itself to them, and to make them happy. All of creation exists thanks to this divine love spending itself. However, the highest of all creatures are those endowed with spirit, able to receive God's love with understanding and to return it freely: angels and human souls. Prayer is the highest achievement of which the human spirit is capable. But it is not merely a human achievement. Prayer is a Jacob's ladder on which the human spirit ascends to God and God's grace descends to people. The stages of prayer are distinguished according to the measure in which the natural efforts of the soul and God's grace participate. When the soul is no longer active by virtue of its own efforts, but is simply a receptacle for grace, one speaks of a mystical life of prayer.

So-called vocal prayer is designated as the lowest stage, prayer that remains within specifically designated spoken forms: the Our Father, the Hail Mary, the rosary, the Divine Office. Of course, "vocal" prayer is not to be understood as simply saying words. If the mere words of a prayer alone are said without the soul's raising itself to God, this is only an outward show and not real prayer. The designated words, however, support the spirit and prescribe to it a fixed path.

Meditative prayer is one stage higher. Here the spirit moves more freely without being bound to specific words. It immerses itself, for example, in the mystery of the birth of Jesus. The spirit's imagination [*Phantasie*] transports it to the grotto in Bethlehem, seeing the child in the manger, the holy parents, the shepherds, and the kings. The intellect ponders the greatness of divine mercy, the emotions are seized by love and thankfulness, the will decides to make itself more worthy of divine love. This is how meditative prayer involves all the soul's powers and, when practiced with faithful persistence, can gradually remake the whole person. However, the Lord has yet another way of rewarding fidelity in meditation: by elevation to a higher manner of praying.

St. Teresa calls the next stage the prayer of quiet or simplicity. Various activities are replaced by a recollection of spiritual energies. The soul is no longer in a position to reflect intellectually or to make definite decisions; she is completely engaged by something she cannot avoid, the presence of her God who is close to her and allows her to rest in him. While the lower prayer stages are accessible to every believer by human effort, albeit aided by the grace of God, we are now standing at the border of the mystical life of grace that cannot be entered by virtue of human energy, for here only God's special favor grants admission.

If the perception of God's presence is already something which totally captivates the soul and gives it a happiness incomparable to any earthly happiness, then this is greatly surpassed by the union with the Lord, which, at first, is usually granted to it for only a very short time.

At this stage of mystical favor many events occur that are also outwardly recognized as extraordinary: *ecstasies* and *visions*. The energy of the soul is so attracted by the supernatural influence that its lower faculties, the senses, lose their effectiveness entirely. The soul no longer sees or hears anything, the body no longer feels pain when injured, and in some cases becomes rigid like someone dead. But the soul lives an intensified life as if it were outside its body. Sometimes the Lord himself appears to it in bodily form, sometimes the Mother of God or an angel or saint. It sees these heavenly forms as if through bodily perception, or also in imagination. Or its intellect is supernaturally enlightened and gains insight into hidden truths. Such private revelations usually have the purpose of teaching souls about their own condition or that of others, of confiding God's intentions to them, and of forming them for a specific task for which God has selected them. They are seldom absent in the lives of saints, though they by no means belong to the essence of holiness. Usually they only appear during a certain phase and later vanish again.

These souls, who have been sufficiently prepared and tested by repeated transitory union with him, by extraordinary illuminations, and at the same time through suffering and various trials, the Lord wishes to bind to himself permanently. He enters into a covenant with them that is called "spiritual betrothal." He expects them to put themselves completely at his service; at the same time, he takes them into safekeeping, cares for them, and is always ready to grant their requests.

Finally, Teresa calls the highest stage of blessedness "spiritual marriage." The extraordinary events have now stopped, but the soul is constantly united with the Lord. She enjoys his presence even in the midst of external activities without being hindered in the least.

The saint had to go through all of these stages during a development that took years before she could account for them herself and give others advice. But the beginnings were during that time of greatest bodily suffering:

> It pleased the heavenly Master to deal with me with such love that he gave me the prayer of quiet. But he often also raised me up to that of union. Unfortunately, I was unfamiliar with either kind. In fact, it would have been useful to me to recognize their value. To be sure, this union did not last long, I believe, hardly as long as one Hail Mary. But it had a great influence on me. I was not yet twenty years old and already believed that I saw the world lying conquered under my feet. I pitied all who had relationships with the world, even if the ties were permitted. I tried with all my strength to be truly present in my soul to Jesus our Lord, our highest Good, our Master. My way of praying was to think about one of the mysteries of his divine life and make a mental image of it. [L, 4, 7]

The effect of her prayer life was an ever-increasing love of God and of souls. If earlier her natural gifts had had an unusual influence on her human surroundings, her supernatural power to love now gave her an almost irresistible force. The first person to experience it was the priest to whom she confessed in Becedas. The insight he had into this pure soul, who blamed herself for innocent little slips with the most bitter regret, disturbed him so much that he himself confessed to his penitent the serious sin in which he had been living for years. Now she could not rest until he had freed himself from these disgraceful fetters. The power of her words and her intercession changed him into a contrite penitent.

After her return to the family home in Avila, the state of the patient got so much worse that there seemed no further hope for her life. Teresa was unconscious for four days. The news of her death spread through the city. Her grave was dug at the Monastery of the Incarnation. The Carmelites of Avila sang a requiem for her. Only her father and siblings continued besieging heaven, and finally she opened her eyes again. At the moment of awakening she spoke some words that implied she had seen some great things during this apparent death. During her last days she admitted that God at that time had shown her heaven and hell, besides her later work in the Order, and the saintly deaths of her father and her friend Juana Suárez, as well as her own. As soon as a slight improvement began, Teresa moved back to her monastery at her urgent request. But she was confined to her bed for several more years, seemed to be crippled forever, and suffered unutterable pain. She herself describes the state of her soul during this time of trial.

> I bore these sufferings with great composure, in fact with joy, except at first when the pain was too severe. What followed seemed to hurt less. I was completely surrendered to the will of God even if he intended to burden me like this forever. It appeared to me that all I wanted was to get healthy so as to withdraw into solitude as my book prescribed. This was difficult in the sick room.... The other sisters wondered at my God-given patience. Without him I truly could not have borne so much with so much joy.
>
> Now I understood how prayer is a blessing. In the first place, it showed me what God's true love was. Next I felt new virtues developing in me that were still very weak.... I never said anything bad about others. Instead, I excused those who were targets of negative gossip, for I reminded myself that I did not want to say nor even liked to hear anything that I would not have liked to hear said about myself. I remained true to this resolution. Sometimes but not often I failed to keep it. I advised the other sisters and people who visited me to do likewise. They assumed these practices. It was soon noticed. It was said that those absent had nothing to fear from me or from my parents and friends.... [L, 6, 3-4]

Teresa suffered for three years without asking for recovery. We do not know why she now changed her mind. She only tells us that she decided to beseech heaven to end her suffering. With this intention, she asked that a Mass be offered and turned toward the saint in whom she had always had unlimited trust, and who owes to her zeal the increased veneration shown him. "I do not know how to think about the Queen of Angels, about all of her pains and cares with the little child Jesus without thanking St. Joseph for the dedication with which he came to the help of both of them" [L, 6, 8]. She ascribed her healing to him.

> Soon he came to my rescue in very obvious ways. This most beloved father and lord of my soul quickly freed me of the weakness and suffering to which my body was consigned.... I don't recall that he ever denied me anything.
>
> St. Joseph permitted his power and goodness to me to become evident. Through him I regained my strength. I stood up, walked, and was free of the paralysis. [see L, 6, 6-8]

## 7. Infidelity

Teresa's generous heart was certainly determined to dedicate the life that had been given to her anew entirely to the service of her beloved Lord. She had no idea that her recovery was to result in dangers, and that when she left the solitary sickroom, there was to be an end for a long time to her excursions among the heights—in fact, that she was to lose again all that she had gained. "My great misfortune was that I found myself in a monastery without an enclosure. Doubtless, the dear nuns could be pleased with the freedom and remain innocent.... But I, weakness itself, would have found it the way to hell had not God with particular grace saved me from this danger" [L, 7, 3].

It was understandable that relatives and friends joyfully welcomed her whose life had been restored, that she was often called into the speakroom, that her lovableness, her animated spirit, her exceptional conversational ability delighted these visitors and drew them to come again and again. All research has concluded that Teresa's association with people in the world, on which she herself looked back with the most bitter repentance for her entire life, was entirely pure and in no way a relapse into worldly frivolity. She had a healthy influence on her visitors and during this time also spoke about nothing more eagerly than divine things. Nevertheless, her remorse is understandable because association with people diverted her from association with God. She lost the taste for prayer, and once she had gone this far, she no longer even thought herself worthy of such a grace.

> Under the pretext of humility, I was afraid of prayer and meditation. I said to myself that, as the most imperfect of persons, it was better for me to do what everyone else was doing and to limit myself to the prescribed verbal prayers. In my condition, which was more suited to the company of the devil, I did not want to pursue so much intimacy with God. I was also afraid of deceiving the whole world. [L, 7, 1]

During this time Teresa impressed the other sisters as a thoroughly first-rate nun.

> In spite of my youth and many relationships to the world, people saw how I sought solitude for reading and for prayer. I often spoke of God. I was fond of having the image of the Savior painted in various places. I had a special place to pray and carefully decorated it with all that could stimulate devotion. I never spread malicious gossip.... [L, 7, 2]

And all that took place "without appearing at all calculating; for I really hated pretense, empty honor, and I believe—God be praised!—

that I never thus offended him. As soon as self-love stirred in my heart, I was so remorseful that the devil lost and I won..." [see L, 7, 1]. But the Lord wanted more from her.

One day while I was talking with someone with whom I had recently become acquainted, God gave me to understand that such acquaintances were not suitable for me and illumined me in my darkness. Our Savior Jesus Christ appeared to me as sad and serious and declared how much I was distressing him. I saw him only with the eyes of my soul, but much more clearly than if I could have seen him with the eyes in my body. His image impressed itself into my spirit so deeply that even now, after more than twenty-six years, it is not erased. Seized by anxiety and confusion, I no longer wanted to receive this person. But to my detriment then, I did not know that the soul can see without the mediation of physical eyes. The devil used my ignorance to tell me this was impossible. He told me that the vision was a delusion, a machination of the devil.... But deep in my heart I still had a secret feeling that what I had seen came from God. But since this did not correspond to my inclinations, I tried to deceive myself. I did not dare to speak with someone about it.... People told me that it was not bad to welcome this person; associating with her would never hurt me, but would be an honor for me. Finally, I gave in. [L, 7, 6-7]

Her father's attitude was a serious warning. He had been allowing his child to lead him on the path of interior prayer and remained faithful to it. Teresa's upright nature could not permit her to leave him under the delusion that she was faithful, too.

I confessed to him, though without indicating the deeper reason, that I had stopped praying. I used only my health as a pretext. Actually, even though I had recovered from the serious illness, I still had to suffer a great deal. But this was not enough to justify myself. One does not need physical strength for prayer, but only love and steadfastness. My father, who loved me tenderly and was deceived by me, believed everything and pitied me. Since he had already progressed far toward perfection, he no longer spent as much time with me. After a short dialogue, he left me with the remark that lengthy lingering is time lost. But I who was losing time in an entirely different way did not see with as sharp an eye. [L, 7, 11-13]

Teresa spent at least one year, possibly longer, in this way. She did not feel at all good about it, and was constantly in great spiritual unrest. Yet again and again she permitted herself to be held back by a false humility. "I do not know how I was able to stand such a state of affairs. Perhaps what kept me going was the hope of taking up praying again. For I still had in my heart the will to return to it again. I was only waiting until I got better. Oh, onto how wicked a path did this insane hope lead me!" [L, 19, 11].

## 8. Return

Teresa was to find deliverance at the deathbed of her father. Upon the news of his serious illness, she was permitted to go to him and be at his side during his last days.

> With him I lost all my happiness and joy. Yet I had the strength to conceal my pain from him. I remained quiet until his death, even though I felt that someone was tearing a piece from my heart as I watched such a precious life being slowly extinguished. But God gave him such a holy death that I cannot thank him enough. It was deeply moving to see the supernatural joy of this good father, to listen to the advice that he gave us after receiving Extreme Unction. He made us promise to commend him to God and to plead for his mercy, to fulfill our duties faithfully, and always to remember how quickly the things of this world pass and perish. With tear-filled eyes, he told us about his pain at not having served God the Lord better and during his last moment rued not having entered the strictest order.
>
> He suffered a great deal, mainly with a piercing pain in his shoulders that gave him not a moment's peace. I remembered his devotion to the mystery of the cross-bearing Savior and told him that God surely wanted to let him feel something of the pain that he himself bore at that time of suffering. This thought gave him such comfort that there no longer came the slightest complaint from his lips. He lay unconscious for three days. However, to our great surprise, on the day of his death God returned him to consciousness and he remained conscious to the end.
>
> In the middle of the creed, which he himself was praying with a clear voice, he gently gave up his spirit. At the same time his features became supernaturally beautiful. He seemed to be resting in the peace of the angels. It seemed to me that he indeed became their brother at the moment of his death because of the purity of his soul and conscience. His confessor (from the order of St. Dominic) told us that he believed that our father had gone straight to heaven. [L, 7, 14-17]]

This Dominican, Fr. Vicente Barrón, made a deep impression on Teresa by the way in which he assisted the dying man. She asked if she could confess to him and gave him complete insight into the state of her soul. Contrary to all others before whom she had up to then accused herself, he recognized at once what she needed and advised her to take up prayer again. "I obeyed and since then I have never given it up again" [L, 7, 17].

But what followed now was not an undisturbed peace but rather years of great spiritual struggles.

> This life that I was leading was very difficult because, in the light of prayer, I saw my errors newly illuminated. On the one hand, God called me; on the other, the world flattered me. Oh, my God, how could I describe all that your compassion did for me during those years or this battle that your love waged against my ingratitude! How am I to find the words to enumerate all the graces that you showered on me? At the moment I was offending you the most you suddenly led my spirit by means of deep rest to the enjoyment of your blessings and your consolations. O my redeemer! It is really true that you knew me. You knew how to punish me in the tenderest and severest way in that you rewarded my errors with good deeds.... My character made me suffer a great deal more when I received blessings after my failures instead of punishment.... In an affliction I would at least have recognized a justified punishment. I would have seen this as a way of doing penance for my many sins. But to find myself showered by new favors, after so shamefully misusing the many already received, was a much greater agony for me. I firmly believe that only those who have some knowledge of and love for God can understand this.... [L, 7, 17-19]

Most souls favored by such graces experience that the interior life usually takes this course. God first draws them to himself by letting them enjoy the supernatural happiness of his beneficent presence, but then tests their fidelity by taking all joys away from them and letting them languish in dryness.

> For three years I was oh so often concerned less with God and good thoughts than with the desire for seeing the end of the hour of prayer. I listened for the bell to finally ring. I would have preferred the most severe penances to the agony of being recollected at the feet of the Savior. The battle I had to endure with the devil and my wicked inclinations to make myself go to the oratory is indescribable. As soon as I entered, a deadly sadness came over me, and it took all my courage to conquer myself and give myself to prayer. Finally, God sent me help. And even if I had to force myself, I more often enjoyed consolations then than on the days when I was in a better mood. [L, 8, 7]

The saint endured these struggles for fourteen years without ever wavering in her faithfulness. Holy Week of the year 1554 brought her release.

> One day as I entered the oratory I saw before me an image of the Savior that someone had placed there for an upcoming feast day.

This image showed our divine Master covered with wounds and with such a peaceful expression that I was moved by it. More than before I apprehended what the Savior had suffered for us. At the same time I experienced my own lack of thankfulness so bitterly that it seemed my heart would break. I fell at the feet of my divine Master and through a stream of tears pleaded with him to give me the strength not to offend him any more. I called on the presence of the holy Magdalene whom I already loved fervently and whose conversion I revered. She came to my help. Without trusting my good intentions, I put my whole trust in God. If I still remember this correctly, I said to him I would not get up until he had heard my plea and I knew for certain that he wanted to grant it. For on that day true life began for me and I never stopped improving. [L, 9, 1-2]

Soon afterward this operation of grace was reinforced by a second similar one.

Someone gave me the *Confessions* of St. Augustine. God granted this, for I never thought of requesting it nor had I ever read it. I had hardly opened this book than I thought that I saw myself in it. With all my strength I commended myself to this great saint.... I had always loved him very much, first because the monastery in which I had been raised followed his rule, and secondly because he was a poor sinner for a long time. I believed that, because God had forgiven him everything, I could also receive my forgiveness....

I cannot describe what happened in my heart when I read the description of his conversion and followed him into the garden where he heard the voice of heaven. It seemed to me as if God were speaking to me. Overcome by regret, I remained dissolved in my tears for a long time. The Lord be eternally praised. He led me from death to life again. My renewed strength made me recognize that he had heard my call and that my tears led him to have mercy on me. [L, 9, 7-9]

## 9. God Alone

Teresa had completed the fortieth year of her life when the Lord rewarded her faithful perseverance and drew her to himself anew, this time forever. According to a comparison that she herself used in her *Life* to portray the various ways of praying, in her view she had up to now operated in her prayer life like a gardener who draws up the water for his garden from a deep well with a great deal of effort. She was most fond of conceiving of the Lord with the help of the imagination [*Phantasie*]— she especially enjoyed seeking him out at the Mount of Olives—and had tried to stay close to him. Now God came to meet her. Like the gardener who has a sufficient supply of water to let it stream forth, she could rest from her efforts. Intellect and memory could cease their activity. In this prayer of quiet, "the will alone is active and, without knowing how, it delivers itself to God like a prisoner for him to chain to himself through his love."

> The soul that surrenders to the divine attraction by this way of praying is raised above its own suffering and receives some knowledge of heavenly glory. It grows, draws near to God, and so becomes stronger. It loses its pleasure in earthly things. Why? It clearly sees that it could not for even a moment enjoy this supernatural joy on earth, that no kingdoms, no realms, no honor, no joys can offer it for even a moment this true happiness that is absolutely the only thing that can satisfy....
>
> Since it has known nothing to surpass this joy, it cherishes no other wish. With complete justification it will say along with St. Peter, "Lord, let us make our home here." [L, 15, 1]

Soon the Lord himself takes over the role of gardener. The soul is raised from *quiet* (theologians usually call this *contemplation*) to *union*.

> In my opinion, this way of praying is a clear union of the entire soul with God. The only leeway God leaves to the faculties is the freedom to recognize the great work he is doing in them. Their only activity is to be occupied with him without being able to do anything else. None of them dares to move. Strong measures would be required to divert them from their divine preoccupation, and, even so, such efforts would never succeed in tearing them away completely. The soul, entirely beside itself and moved by the sweetest rapture, would like its voice to intone hymns of praise, that everything in it could extol the superabundance of its happiness. [L, 16, 2-3]

Often enough, such hymns of praise have streamed from the lips of the saint.

At the beginning of her mystical life the duration of the union was very short, Teresa says hardly as long as one Hail Mary. But its effect was astounding.

> By one single visit, no matter how short, God changed the face, the appearance of the mystical garden.... Unaware [of what happened] the soul sees itself transformed. It finds I do not know what powers to do great things. At the same time it recognizes that it could not in many years acquire those virtues that the Lord has just given it, and it feels a humility beginning in itself that is much more profound than anything beforehand....
>
> When God the Lord raises a soul to this stage of prayer, he requires nothing more from her than a simple consent to the graces he is giving her and a full surrender to the will of his divine wisdom. He intends to dispose of her as he does of his property. [L, 17, 1-3]

Frequently the union increases to *rapture*. Overpowered by the force of grace and supernatural joy, the soul loses the use of its lower powers and the control of its own body.

During rapture it is almost always impossible to resist the supernatural power of attraction. The soul must have more decisiveness and courage than in the prior states. For when it is in these raptures, one feels oneself carried away without knowing where one is going or what is going to become of one, and our weak nature feels during this otherwise so delightful moment I cannot say what dread. Not only is the soul carried away, but sometimes the body also itself follows this movement, so that it no longer touches the floor. Should I want to be on solid ground again, I would feel under my feet astounding powers lifting me up against my will. It was a dreadful struggle. I remained as though annihilated and in fact I saw clearly that if God wills something, all resistance to his omnipotence amounts to nothing.

The effects of such an extraordinary favor are great. First, it demonstrates to us God's omnipotence and teaches us that we are the masters of neither our bodies nor our souls, but that we have a divine Master who does what he wants with them. The other effect is a rare detachment that I have no words to describe. One truly feels like a stranger to things here below. Because they are vying with each other, promises and heroic resolutions come from these things; lively desires, frank aversion to the world; a clear glimpse into its nothingness. Finally, this prayer leaves behind in the soul such great love that it could perish, not from pain, but from the tears of joy that it pours out.

…One hour's ecstasy or even shorter is sufficient to make the soul the mistress of itself and of all things and to give it a freedom in which it no longer recognizes even itself.…

What power is comparable to the power of a soul that has been raised by God to these heights, and sees beneath it the things of the world without in the least being governed by them! How confused it is about the time when it clung to them! How amazed it is by its blindness! How greatly is it concerned over those who still live in the same darkness! It would like to raise its voice to show them their error. It would like to break their chains and tear them from the prison of this life where it itself had been locked up. But then when it looks at itself, it not only sees the cobwebs or the great sins, but also the tiniest dust specks or the tiniest spots.… If on the one hand it contemplates the endless holiness of its God, it is blinded by his light. On the other hand, if it looks at itself, its eye seems to find her who is covered with the mud of her misery.… O happy, a thousand times happy, the soul whom God through ecstasy raises to the knowledge of the truth. [see L, 20, 3-8; 20, 25-29; 21, 1]

These recollections reveal to us the whole nature of the saint: the sensitivity of her conscience that with bitter regret accused itself when no one else could find a spot on her; the ardor of her love that made her ready to make any sacrifice for the glory of God; her concern over souls whom she wanted with all her might to rescue from ruin and to lead to the peace of the Lord. But before she was permitted to do great things as God's chosen instrument, she still had to taste the most bitter pains.

## 10. New Tests

The first difficulty arose from her own ignorance of mystical theology. In her deep humility, she could not imagine how an unworthy person (as in her opinion she was) could be so richly laden with such extraordinary favors. Of course, as long as the favors during prayer lasted she could not doubt their authenticity. But in between she was plagued by fears that these mystical states were deceptions of the devil. On the basis of her experience, Teresa later said again and again how necessary it is for a soul that is going the way of the interior life to have the guidance of a learned and enlightened spiritual director. Fr. Vicente Barrón, who had so charitably stood by her after the death of her father, had been called away from Avila some time earlier. In her need, upon the advice and through the mediation of a dear friend, the pious nobleman Francisco de Salcedo, she turned to Gaspar Daza, a priest who was considered throughout the city to be as holy as he was learned. His evaluation was devastating. He interpreted all of her favors during prayer as deceptions of the devil and advised her to cease entirely what she had been doing up to now. The saint fell into the utmost distress—showered by favors from heaven while at the same time, according to the theological expert, in the gravest danger, and directed to pull back from the supernatural influences! There appeared one more way out of her distress. A short time earlier a college of the Society of Jesus had been started in Avila. Teresa, who had the greatest admiration for the new order, heard this with joy, but up to now had not dared to speak with one of the greatly renowned fathers. Now she took refuge in them, and this was her deliverance. Fr. Juan de Prádanos completely reassured her about the origin of her mystical states and advised her to continue on this path. He only found it necessary that she make herself worthy of the favors by strict mortifications. As she said, "mortification" was at that time a word virtually unknown to her. But with her characteristic decisiveness, she took up the suggestion and began to accustom herself to severe penances. Recognizing that her weak health would not be able to stand such a severe life, P. Prádanos easily helped her with this. "Without doubt, my daughter," he said, "God sends you so many illnesses in order to make up for those mortifications that you do not practice. So do not be afraid. Your mortifications cannot hurt you" [see L, 24, 6].

And in fact Teresa's health improved because of this new lifestyle. Even though her new spiritual director had no doubt about the heavenly origin of her favors during prayer, he still thought it a good idea to impose on her some constraint in her manner of meditating and to instruct her in resisting the stream of favors. But even this restriction was soon to be lifted again. St. Francis Borgia visited the Jesuit college and to get his evaluation, Fr. Prádanos asked him to speak with Teresa. She herself writes about this:

> I let him...know the state of my soul. After listening to me, he told me that everything happening in me came from the spirit of God. He called my behavior good so far. But he said that in the future I should offer no more resistance. He advised me always to begin my prayers by meditating on one of the mysteries of the passion. If then without my assistance the Lord transported my spirit into a supernatural state, I should surrender to his guidance.... He left me completely consoled. [L, 24, 3]

If the saint herself was calmed by such weighty testimony, it was not so in her surroundings. Despite of the testimony of St. Francis Borgia, and despite the sympathetic guidance she found, soon after the recall of Fr. Prádanos, in his very young but saintly confrere, Fr. Baltasar Alvarez, her devoted friends did not stop worrying about her. They asked others for advice, and soon everyone in the city was talking about the unusual phenomena at the Monastery of the Incarnation and warning the young Jesuit not to let himself be deceived by his penitent. Even though he placed no credence in these voices, he did think it advisable to pose Teresa some difficult tests. He denied her solitude, and once withheld Holy Communion from her for twenty days. She submitted to all orders. But it was no wonder that unrest once more arose in her heart also, since everyone else doubted her or appeared to doubt her. Her deliverance was the goodness of the Lord who calmed her again and again, who enraptured her right in the middle of the mandatory conversations, since solitary prayer was taken from her. Above all, he strengthened her to persist faithfully in the way of obedience no matter how hard it was. Her reward was new, continually greater favors. She felt the presence of the Savior by her side often for entire days. At first he came to her invisibly, but later also in a visible form.

> The Savior almost always appeared to me visibly in risen form. When I saw him in the holy Host, he was in this transfigured form. Sometimes when I was tired or sad, he showed me his wounds to encourage me. He also appeared to me hanging on the cross. I saw him in the garden; finally, I saw him carrying the cross. When he appeared to me in such a form, it was, I repeat, because of a need in

my soul or for the consolation of various other persons; still his body was always glorified. [L, 29, 4]

These appearances increased Teresa's love and strengthened her in the certainty that it was none other than the Lord who was visiting her with his favors. So it must have been all the more painful to her when, in the absence of Fr. Alvarez, another confessor ordered her to send the "evil spirit" away each time it appeared by making the sign of the cross and a gesture of contempt. She also obeyed this command. But at the same time she fell at the feet of the Lord and pleaded with him for forgiveness: "Oh Savior, you know when I act like this toward you that I do it only out of love for you because I want to submit obediently to him whom you have appointed in your Church to take your place for me." And Jesus calmed her. "Be comforted, my daughter, you do well to obey. I will reveal the truth" [see L, 29, 6].

In this obedience toward the church, the saint herself had always seen the surest criterion that a soul was on the right way.

> I know for certain that God would never allow the devil to delude a soul that mistrusts itself and whose faith is so strong that it was prepared to endure a thousand deaths for the sake of one single article of faith. God blesses this noble disposition of the soul by strengthening its faith and making it ever more fiery. This soul carefully tries to transform itself so that it is completely in line with the teachings of the church and for this purpose asks questions of anyone who could elucidate them. It hangs on so tightly to the church's creeds that all conceivable revelations—even if it saw heaven opened—could never make it vacillate in its faith even in the most minute article taught by the church....
>
> Should a soul not find in itself this powerful faith or its delight in devotion not contribute to increasing its dependence on the holy church, then I say that the soul is on a path filled with danger. The spirit of God only flows into things that are in agreement with the holy Scriptures. If there had been the slightest deviation, I would have been convinced that these things came from the author of lies. [L, 25, 12-13]

That after each new favor she grew in humility and love must have pacified the saint herself, and must also have been an unmistakable sign to the enlightened men of the spirit of the disposition of her soul.

During that time of unusual demonstrations of grace and of the most severe tests, Teresa also received a visible sensory image of the glowing love that pierced her heart. "I saw beside me at my left side an angel in a physical form.... Because of his flaming face, he seemed to belong to that lofty choir made up only of fire and love.... I saw a long golden dart in his hands the end of which glowed like fire. From time to time the angel pierced my heart with it. When he pulled it out again, I was entirely inflamed with love for God" [L, 29, 13]. The heart of the saint, which has been preserved in the monastery of Alba and remains intact to this day, bears a long, deep wound.

## 11. Works for the Lord

One who loves feels compelled to do something for the beloved. Teresa, who even as a child showed herself to be boldly decisive and ready to act, burned with the desire to show the Lord her love and thankfulness by action. As a nun in a contemplative monastery, she seemed to be cut off from all outer activity. So she at least wanted to do as much as possible to make herself holy. With the permission of her confessor (Fr. Alvarez) and her highest superior in the Order, she took a vow always to do what would be most pleasing to God. To protect her from uncertainty and from qualms of conscience, the text was later changed to read that her confessor was to decide what would be perfect at any given time.

But a soul so full of love could not be satisfied with caring for its own salvation and making the Lord happy by its own perfection. One day she was transported into hell by a horrible vision. "I immediately understood that God wanted to show me the place that the devil had reserved for me and that I deserved for my sins. It lasted hardly a moment. But even if I live for many more years, I will never be able to forget it" [L, 32, 1]. She recognizes what God's goodness has preserved her from. "The superscription for my life should read 'the mercy of God.'" But countless other people are constantly subject to the dangers that she herself had escaped. "How could I find one day of rest with such an outlook? How could I live in peace while so many souls were being lost?" It was at the time when Germany was torn by schism, France was tearing itself to pieces in wars of religion, and all Europe was confused by false doctrines. "Brokenhearted, as though I could do something or as if I myself were someone, I embraced the feet of the Lord, shed bitter tears, and asked him to remedy such evil. I would gladly have sacrificed a thousand lives to save one of these misguided souls. But how could a poor woman like me serve the cause of her divine Master?" [W, 1, 2]. During such reflections, there occurred to her the thought of freeing herself from the mitigated Rule of her monastery:

> ...so that she could rest entirely in God like the saints, the hermits who had preceded her. Since she could not, as she would have liked, extol God's mercy throughout the entire world, she at least wanted to gather some selected souls around her who would dedicate themselves to poverty, withdrawal, constant prayer, and the strictness of the primitive Rule. Already full of this thought, which

was not simply fantasy but a firm decision, she conceived of how she would surround herself with a small band of noble souls who were ready to join her in doing what was most perfect. She considered how she might pray day and night to be a constant support to those destined to save souls…. It seemed to her as though she were already in the situation, which appeared to her as paradise. She saw herself already living in a little house clad in sackcloth, enclosed behind the walls, only occupied with prayer, and hurrying with her companions to serve the most Beloved.[6]

It was not to be too long before this lovely dream was to become reality.

## 12. Saint Joseph's of Avila, the First Monastery of the Reform

A small group of nuns and visitors present for worship on the feast of the Blessed Virgin of Mount Carmel on July 16, 1560, were discussing the obstacles to a life of prayer presented by the large number of nuns living in the monastery and the many visitors. María de Ocampo, a young relative of the saint and a celebrated beauty, suggested that someone should establish a monastery in which the life of the ancient hermits could be revived. In all seriousness she offered her dowry for this. The next day Teresa told her trusted friend Doña Guiomar de Ulloa (a young widow who like her led a life of prayer under the strict direction of Fr. Baltasar Alvarez) of this conversation. Doña Guiomar enthusiastically took up the idea. But what was decisive was that the Lord himself was calling for the project. "He assured me that he would be very well-served in a monastery I might found, that this house would become a star shedding the brightest light. God added that, even though they had lost some of their earlier enthusiasm, the orders were nevertheless of great service to him. What would the world be if there were no more monasteries?" [see L, 32, 11]. According to the will of the Lord, the new house was to be consecrated to St. Joseph.

Now Teresa no longer hesitated. First she turned to her confessor. He made his consent dependent on the consent of the provincial of the Carmelites, Fr. Angel de Salazar.[7] This consent was easier to get than expected because of the mediation of Doña Guiomar. Three very devout religious, whose advice Teresa sought, gave encouraging replies: Jesuit Francis Borgia, Dominican Luis Beltrán, and Franciscan Peter of Alcántara. Now the next task was to find a house. But before that could happen the public scented Teresa's plans, and this aroused a storm of indignation against her and her friends. One can certainly understand that the nuns of the Monastery of the Incarnation would take it as malicious arrogance for one of their own to want to leave their house to live in greater perfection than the community in which she had been formed. And people in the city shared this view. The two women received their first strong support from the scholarly and highly respected Dominican, Fr. Pedro Ibáñez. When the provincial withdrew his consent under the pressure of Teresa's sisters and compelled the saint to inaction, her friends continued with the work of preparation: Doña Guiomar, directed by Fr. Ibáñez, Don Francisco de Salcedo, and Gaspar Daza (the two who had once by their doubt caused her so much soul searching, but were now entirely won over to her). A little house was discovered. Her brother-in-law, Juan de Ovalle, the husband of her youngest sister Juana, who herself had been raised in the Monastery of the Incarnation and loved Teresa greatly, bought it and moved in to protect it until it could be given over to its real purpose.

It seemed like a great hindrance to her plans when the saint received the surprising order from her Father Provincial to go to the palace of Duchess Luisa de la Cerda in Toledo, because this influential lady sought the comfort of the saint in her grief over the death of her husband. Teresa's friends hated to see her leave Avila. But the stay in Toledo was to be richly blessed. Doña Luisa became a powerful and faithful patroness of the reform. In the circle of women and girls that gathered around Teresa at the palace to seek her advice, there was someone soon to be one of her strongest supporters, the young María de Salazar (later María of St. Joseph, prioress of Seville). Above all, Teresa found the leisure here to write the story of her interior life, a project given to her the previous year by Fr. Ibáñez. This book was to make her name known in all Catholic lands, and down through the centuries would become a guide for countless people.

Even in regard to her foundation in Avila the time was not wasted. In the house of the Duchess de la Cerda, she was sought out by María of Jesus, a Carmelite from Granada who had reform ideas similar to Teresa's and wanted to talk them over with her. She also found occasion for a consultation with St. Peter of Alcántara, who on an earlier occasion had tested the state of her soul and consoled her greatly. Now he encouraged her to found the Monastery of St. Joseph without an income, as the primitive Rule prescribed.

Teresa was permitted to return to Avila only in June of 1562, after a six-month stay. Good news that came on the day of her arrival awaited her there: the papal brief that permitted Doña Guiomar and her mother to establish a Carmelite monastery according to the primitive Rule, placing it under the jurisdiction of the diocesan bishop, giving it the same rights as other monasteries of the same order, and prohibiting anyone from disturbing it in any way. Teresa's name was not mentioned in the document. By a lucky coincidence, Peter of Alcántara was just then in Avila—for the last time, for he died shortly thereafter. His efforts succeeded in winning the bishop of Avila, Don Alvaro de Mendoza, for the foundation. From then on the bishop was one of the most enthusiastic promoters of the reform.

The illness of her brother-in-law, Juan de Ovalle, resulted in her gaining the permission of her provincial to move into his house, her future monastery, to care for him. This gave her the opportunity to supervise the construction personally. When the workers left the house, the patient was also healed and the monastery could become what it was meant to be. Now the most important thing was to find suitable living stones for the new foundation. There were four postulants about whom the Holy Mother herself said, "My first daughters were four orphans without dowries, but great servants of God. I found just what I had wished for, because my most ardent desire was that the first to enter would by their example be suitable building blocks of the spiritual edifice, would fulfill our intentions and lead lives of contemplation and perfection" [see L, 36, 6]. On August 24, the feast of St. Bartholomew, these first four Carmelites of the reform arrived at the little monastery where the saint awaited them. The friends who had helped to make the foundation made their appearance. By commission of the Bishop of Avila, Gaspar Daza celebrated the first Mass and reserved the Blessed Sacrament in the chapel. Thereby the foundation was completed. Then Teresa clothed her daughters in the robe of the discalced Carmelites ("discalced," or "without shoes," because instead of shoes they wore the footwear of the poor, sandals made of hemp).[8] Their habits and scapulars were made of coarse brown frieze; the mantles of white frieze; the toques of linen; and over them for the time being they wore the white novice's veil. Overjoyed, the mother remained behind with her daughters in the quiet of the holy place when the visitors departed. But people did not leave her in peace for long. The rumor of the accomplished foundation quickly spread to the entire city. The opposition stirred up all the townspeople. A monastery without any income would consume the alms of the poor. The prioress of the Incarnation, pressured by the indignant sisters, sent Teresa an order to return to her monastery immediately. The Saint obeyed at once. She left the four novices behind under the protection of St. Joseph and the direction of the oldest, Ursula of the Saints. On August 26 the city's municipal judge summoned the mayor and the cathedral chapter to a meeting in the city hall. The consensus was that the monastery was to be suppressed, and the municipal judge himself went there. But Teresa's young daughters did not allow themselves to be intimidated. When threatened with force, they answered through the grille, "...You may use force. But...such actions are judged here on earth by his Majesty Philip II, and in heaven by another judge, whom you should fear a great deal more, the almighty God, the champion of the oppressed." The city magistrate left without doing anything and called another, larger gathering for the next day. In an inflammatory speech he explained that this foundation was an innovation and as such suspect. The maintenance of the nuns would excessively burden the nobility of Avila. Opening the house without the permission of the city was illegal. Therefore, one must conclude that it be suppressed. The speaker already had the majority on his side when a Dominican asked to speak. It was Fr. Domingo Báñez who had only been in Avila for a short time, but was famous for his scholarship. He did not know Teresa, but his love for justice impelled him to become a spokesman for her cause.

> Is it a sufficient reason to destroy something because it is new? Were not all societies of orders innovations when they arose from the bosom of the Church? And when our Lord and God founded the Church, did his work not bear the mark of innovation? ...This newly founded monastery of Carmelites is a reform of the ancient community. It picks up what has fallen. It renews a weakened *Rule*. It strives for the formation of people for the glory of the holy faith. For these reasons it must not only be tolerated by the powers of the state and of the city, but favored and protected.
>
> ...How can anyone believe that poor women confined in a corner who pray to God for us could become such a heavy burden and a danger to the people? ...The frightening specter that is the entire cause of the disturbance in Avila is that of four humble, peace-loving Carmelites living at the outermost end of a suburb.... It seems to me of little use to Avila to call a council for such an insignificant reason.
>
> The existence of the monastery is inviolable, since the Most Reverend Bishop Alvaro de Mendoza has taken it under his protection and the Holy See has given its approval in a brief, against which all of Avila can do nothing.... [cf. L, 36, 15]

In response to his speech, the gathering broke up and the little monastery was rescued. However, it took several more months of negotiations and the sacrificial efforts of all the friends to overcome the rest of the hindrances. Finally, on December 5, 1562, the provincial Angel de Salazar[9] gave Teresa permission to go to her daughters. She was even allowed to take along four nuns from the Monastery of the Incarnation. In overflowing thanks to the Lord, she once again consecrated herself and her little religious family to his service. Now she and those accompanying her put on the rough habit of the reform and exchanged their shoes for coarse sandals. At the same time, in order to bury all reminders of rank and status in the world, they gave up their family names and chose a noble title that came from heaven. From that day on, Teresa de Ahumada was called *Teresa of Jesus*.

The chaplain, Julián de Avila, the first confessor at St. Joseph's and a faithful assistant to the saint in the work of reform, wrote a history of the founding of this house after the saint's death. He gives us a picture of heavenly life in this solitude: "God wanted...to have a house where he could recreate, a dwelling for his consolation. He wanted a garden with flowers, not those flowers that grow on the earth, but those that unfold in heaven..., a flower garden with these selected souls in whose midst he could take his repose, to whom he could disclose his secrets and open his heart." "Because our Lord and Savior has so many enemies and so few friends, at least the latter must be very good," said the saint herself [see W, 1, 2]. And she educated the young souls entrusted into her hands to be such good friends of the Lord. Girls of youthful beauty, rich and sparkling with talent, rushed to St. Joseph's in order to discard all finery, in order to consecrate themselves to the Lord in unlimited self-forgetfulness and humble submission. Postulants also came without any dowries and were received just as joyfully, in fact, even more lovingly. For the Holy Mother was concerned with having the real spirit of the order in her house, not with external goods. Soon the number reached thirteen, which Teresa originally did not want to exceed. (Later it was raised to twenty.) She regulated life in the house with the greatest wisdom.[10] Each sister received an office in which she served the requirements of the little monastic family. The day was strictly apportioned between work and prayer. And this work, which was to contribute support, had to be simple and modest, not giving rise to pride, and thereby preserving their recollection in God. The work was carried out in solitude and silence. Only during the hour of recreation did the sisters come together in heartfelt and spontaneous conversation. Teresa made this hour into a required practice and set great store by it, to allow the spirit the relaxation that nature demands and to give sufficient opportunity for the practice of sisterly love. But even during this hour of recreation there was no idleness. During lively conversation or joyful song, busy hands raced as fast as they could.

Her little family's spirit was Teresa's greatest reward for all her efforts and sacrifice. She herself stood in wonder before her daughters:

> Oh how I recognize all the superiorities of these sisters over me! No sooner had God given them some understanding, some love, than for his sake they disdained the lives to which they used to be attached and sacrificed themselves for him. They find their delight in solitude. All their happiness lies in thoughts of making progress in serving God. Their blessedness is to live alone with him. Many of them spent their youth in the vanity of the world. They intended to find their happiness there and to make decisions according to the world's standards. But precisely these are the most joyful. God rewards them with true joy for the false delights they have left for him. I cannot say how much comfort I feel living in the company of such innocent souls who have renounced everything. [see L, 35, 12]

The saint also had no other desire than to live in this separation from the world with her little family, to lead them ever more deeply into the spirit of prayer, into the heroic exercise of virtues—humility, obedience, complete giving of oneself, poverty, the most heartfelt love for God and for people—and to consecrate with them this whole life of prayer, sacrifice, voluntary penance (on which, however, she set a wise limit and so obviated an unhealthy enthusiasm) to the glory of God and his church, for the salvation of souls and as a support for priests who were doing battle with the great errors of the time. But she was not to conclude her life in the quiet of St. Joseph's.

### 13. Spread of the Reform

Again, it was her burning desire for the salvation of souls that led Teresa to new action. One day a Franciscan from the missions visited her and told her about the sad spiritual and moral condition of people in heathen lands. Shaken, she withdrew into her hermitage in the garden. "I cried to the Savior, I pleaded with him for the means of winning souls for him because the evil enemy robs him of so many. I asked him to help himself a little by my prayers, because that was all I could offer him" [F, 1, 7]. After petitioning like this for many days, the Lord appeared to her and spoke the comforting words, "Wait a little while, my daughter, and you will see great things" [F, 1, 8]. Six months later came the fulfillment of this promise.

In the spring of the year 1567 she received news of an upcoming visit to Spain by the Carmelite General, Giovanni Battista Rossi (Rubeo). "This was something most unusual. The generals of our order always have been situated in Rome. None had ever come to Spain before" [F, 2, 1]. The nun who had left her monastery and founded a new one had reason to be afraid of the arrival of her highest superior. He had the power to destroy her work. With the consent of the bishop of Avila who had jurisdiction of her house, Teresa invited the general to visit. He came, and Teresa gave him a completely candid account of the entire history of the foundation. What he saw convinced him of the spirit that ruled in this little monastery and he was moved to tears. It was evident that here was a perfect realization of the goal for which he had come to Spain. He was considering a reform of the entire Order, a return to the old traditions, but he had not risked proceeding as radically as Teresa. King Philip II had called him to Spain to renew discipline in the monasteries of his land. Fr. Rubeo had found little friendly reception in other places. Now he confided his concerns to Teresa. For her part, she responded with love and a daughter's trust. When he departed from Avila, he left Teresa with permits to found additional women's monasteries of the reform. All these monasteries were to be directly under the general.

No provincial was to have the right to hinder their foundation or to involve himself in their affairs. When he returned to Madrid, Fr. Rubeo spoke enthusiastically to the king about Teresa and her work. Philip II asked for her prayers and those of her daughters, and was from then on the most powerful friend and protector of the reform. After returning to Rome, the Father General gave the saint even more power: to found two monasteries for men according to the primitive Rule if she could obtain the permission of the present provincial and that of his predecessor. This permission was obtained for her by the bishop of Avila, who himself had been the first to express the wish for monasteries of friars of the reform. Teresa now found herself in an unusual position. Instead of a quiet little monastery to which she could retreat with a few selected souls, she was now to found an entire order for men and women. "And only a poor, unshod Carmelite was there to accomplish this, even though furnished with permits and the best wishes, but without any means for initiating the work and without any other support than that of the Lord..." [F, 2, 6]. But this support sufficed. Before long, what was most important for a monastery of men appeared: the first friars. While she was making the first foundation for nuns in Medina del Campo, the prior of the Carmelite monastery of the mitigated rule there, Fr. Antonio de Heredia, energetically stood by Teresa's side. When she told him of her plan, he declared himself ready to be the first male discalced Carmelite. Teresa was surprised and not absolutely happy, because she did not fully credit him with having the strength to sustain the primitive Rule. However, he stayed firm in his decision. A few days later, a companion for him appeared who was most satisfactory to the saint: a young Carmelite at that time called John of St. Matthias, who from his early youth had lived a life of prayer and the strictest self-denial. He had gained the permission of his superior to follow the primitive Rule personally. Not satisfied with this, he was thinking of becoming a Carthusian. Teresa persuaded him, instead, to become the living cornerstone of the Carmelite Order of the primitive Rule.

Some time later a little house in Duruelo, a hamlet between Avila and Medina del Campo, was offered to her for the planned foundation. It was in miserable condition, but neither Teresa nor the two fathers were taken aback by it. Fr. Antonio still needed some time to end his priorship and put all his affairs in order. In the meantime, Fr. John joined Holy Mother to acquaint himself with the spirit and rule of life of the reform under her personal direction. On September 20, 1568 he went to Duruelo, having been clothed by Teresa in the habit of the reform, which she herself had made for him. As the Holy Mother had anticipated, he divided the single room of the pitiful little hut into two cells, an attic room into the choir, a vestibule into a chapel where he celebrated the first Mass the next morning. Soon he was considered a saint by the peasants in the neighborhood. On November 27, Fr. Antonio joined him. Together they now committed themselves to the primitive Rule and changed their names. From then on they were called Anthony of Jesus[Antonio de Jesús] and John of the Cross [Juan de la Cruz].

A few months later the Holy Mother could visit them and get to know their way of life. She says about this:

> I came there during Lent in the year 1569. It was morning. Father Antonio in his always cheerful mood was sweeping the doorway to the church. "What does this mean, my father," I said, "and where is your self-respect?" ... "Oh, cursed be the time when I paid attention to that," he answered chuckling. I went into the chapel and was seized by the spirit of fervor and poverty with which God had filled it. I was not the only one so moved. Two merchants with whom I was friendly and who had accompanied me from Medina del Campo looked at the house with me. They could only weep. There were crosses and skulls everywhere. I will never forget a little wooden cross over a holy water font to which an image of the Savior had been glued. This image was made of simple paper; however, it flooded me with more devotion than if it had been very valuable and beautifully made. The choir, once an attic room, was raised in the middle so that the fathers could comfortably pray the Office. But one still had to bow deeply when entering. At both sides of the church, there were two little hermitages where they could only sit or lie down and even so their heads would touch the roof. The floor was so damp that they had to put straw on it. I learned that the fathers, instead of going to sleep after matins, retreated to these little hermitages and meditated there until prime. In fact, they once were praying in such recollection that when snow fell on them through the slats in the roof, they did not notice it at all, and returned to the choir without it occurring to them even to shake their robes. [F, 14, 7]

Duruelo was the cradle of the male branch of the reformed Carmel. It spread vigorously from there, always directed by the Holy Mother's prayer and illuminating suggestions, but nevertheless relatively independent. The humble little John of the Cross, the great saint of the church, inspired it with the spirit. But he was entirely a person of prayer, of penance. Others took on the external direction. Besides Fr. Antonio, there were the enthusiastic Italians, Fr. Mariano and Fr. Nicolás Doria. But, above all, the most faithful support for the Holy Mother during her last years was, as she was convinced, the choice instrument of the reform, the youthful, brilliantly gifted Fr. Jerónimo Gracián of the Mother of God.

Teresa herself had hardly any time for quiet monastic life after she left the peace of St. Joseph's upon founding the first daughter house in

Medina del Campo. She was called now here, now there, to establish new houses of the reform. Despite her always fragile health and increasing age, she indefatigably undertook the most difficult journeys as often as the Lord's service required. Everywhere there were hard battles to endure: Sometimes there were difficulties with the spiritual and civil authorities, sometimes the lack of a suitable house and the basic necessities of life, sometimes disagreements with upper-class founders who made impossible demands of the monasteries. When finally all obstacles had been overcome and everything organized so that the true life of Carmel could begin, she who had done it all had, without pause, to move on to new tasks. The only consolation she had was that a new garden was blooming for the Lord to enjoy.

## 14. Prioress at the Monastery of the Incarnation

While the spiritual gardens of Mother Teresa were spreading their lovely fragrance over all of Spain, the Monastery of the Incarnation, her former home, was in a sad state. Income had not increased in proportion to the number of nuns, and since they were used to living comfortably and not (as in the reformed Carmel) to finding their greatest joy in holy poverty, discontent and slackening of spirit spread. In the year 1570, Fr. Fernández of the Order of St. Dominic came to this house. He was the apostolic visitator entrusted by Pope Pius V with examining the disciplinary state of monasteries in Castile. Since he had already become thoroughly acquainted with some monasteries of the reform, the contrast must have shocked him. He thought of a radical remedy. By the authority of his position, he named Mother Teresa as prioress of the Monastery of the Incarnation and ordered her to return to Avila at once to assume her position. In the midst of her work for the reform, she now had to undertake a task that for all intents and purposes appeared impossible. Exhorted by the Lord himself, she declared her readiness. However, with the agreement of Fr. Fernández, she gave a written statement that she personally would continue to follow the primitive Rule. One can imagine the vehement indignation of the nuns who were to have a prioress sent to them—one not elected by them—a sister of theirs who had left them eight years earlier and whom they considered an adventuress, a mischief-maker. The storm broke as the provincial led her into the house. The provincial, Fr. Angel de Salazar,[11] could not make himself heard in the noisy gathering. The "Te Deum" that he intoned was drowned out by the sounds of indignation. Teresa's goodness and humility finally brought about enough quiet for the sisters to go to their cells and to tolerate her presence in the house.

They were saving the decisive declarations for the first chapter meeting. But how amazed they were when they entered the chapter

room at the sound of the bell to see in the prioress' seat the statue of
our dear Lady, the Queen of Carmel, with the keys to the monastery in
her hands and the new prioress at her feet. Their hearts were conquered
even before Teresa began to speak and in her indisputably loving manner presented to them how she conceived and intended to conduct her
office. In a short time, under her wise and temperate direction, above
all by the influence of her character and conduct, the spirit of the house
was renewed. Her greatest support in this was Fr. John of the Cross,
whom she called to Avila as confessor for the monastery.

This time of greatest expenditure of energy when Teresa, along with
being prioress of the Monastery of the Incarnation, retained the spiritual direction of her eight reformed monasteries, was also a time of the
greatest attestation of grace. At that time she had a vision that she herself described as a "spiritual marriage." On November 18, 1572, the Lord
appeared to her during Holy Communion. "He offered me his right
hand and spoke, 'See this nail. It is the sign of our union. From this day
on you are my bride. Up to now you had not earned it. But now you will
not only see me as your Creator, your King, your God, but from now on
you will care for my honor as my true bride. My honor is yours; your glory
is mine'" [ST, 31]. From that moment on, she found herself united bliss-
fully with the Lord, a union that remained with her for the entire last
decade of her life, her own life mortified, "full of the inexpressible joy
of having found her true rest, and of the sense that Jesus Christ was living in her."[12] She characterized as the first result of this union "such a
complete forgetfulness of self that it truly seems as if this soul had lost its
own being. It no longer recognizes itself. It no longer thinks about
heaven for itself, about life, about honor. The only thing she cares about
any longer is the honor of God" [C, 7, 3, 2]. The second result is an inner
desire for suffering, a desire, however, that no longer disturbs her soul
as earlier. She desires with such fervor that God's will be fulfilled in her
that everything that pleases the divine Master seems good to her. If he
wants her to suffer, she is happy; if he does not, his will be done.

> But the following surprised me the most. This soul whose life
> has been martyrdom, because of her strong desire to enjoy the vi-
> sion of God, has now become so consumed by the wish to serve him,
> to glorify his name, and to be useful to other souls that, far from
> wishing to die, she would like to live for many years in the greatest
> suffering....
> In this soul there is no more interior pain or dryness, but only a
> sweet and constant joy. Should she for a short time be less attentive
> to the presence of God, he himself immediately awakens her. He
> works to bring her to complete perfection and imparts his doctrines
> in a completely hidden way in the midst of such a deep peace that it
> reminds me of the building of Solomon's temple. Actually, the soul

becomes the temple of God where only God alone and the soul mutually delight in each other in greatest quiet. [C, 7, 3, 6-11]

## 15. Doing Battle for Her Life's Work

The greatest grace that can befall a soul was probably necessary to strengthen the saint for the storm that was soon to break over the reform. Even during her term as prioress, she had to resume her journeys of foundation and leave a vicaress in charge in Avila. At the end of her years as prioress it was only with some effort that she stopped the nuns from re-electing her. Those who had so struggled against her assuming the position clung to her with such great love. Her humility and goodness, her superior intelligence and wise moderation in this case had been able to bridge the rift between the "calced" and the "discalced." Her spiritual sons were not so lucky. They had founded new monasteries in addition to the two for which the general of the Order, Fr. Rubeo, had previously given Teresa authorization. They had the permission of the apostolic visitator from Andalusia, Fr. Vargas, but no arrangement with the Order's superiors. Their extraordinary penances (which often caused the saint herself concern) and their zeal soon aroused the admiration of the people. This, along with the apostolic visitator's evident preference for the monasteries of the reform, made those not of the reform fear they themselves would soon be pushed entirely into the background, even that the reform might be imposed on the entire Order. Their envoys turned the general in Rome completely against the discalced as disobedient and as agitators. To suppress their "revolt," Fr. Tostado, a Portuguese Carmelite with special authority, was sent to Spain. A clash between the two branches of the Order ensued, which must have filled the heart of the humble and peace-loving Holy Mother with the greatest pain. In addition, it appeared that her entire work was threatened. She herself was called "a gadabout" by the new papal nuncio in Spain, "disobedient, ambitious, who presumes to teach others like a doctor of the church despite the prohibition of Saint Paul." She was ordered to choose one of the reformed monasteries as her permanent residence and to make no further trips. How grateful she would have been for the quiet in the monastery of Toledo, which Fr. Gracián suggested to her, had there not been such a hostile design behind the command! All the monasteries of the reform were prohibited from taking in novices, condemning them to extinction. Her beloved sons were reviled and persecuted. Fr. John of the Cross, who had always kept himself far from all conflict, was even secretly abducted and kept in humiliating confinement in the monastery of the calced in Toledo. He was cruelly abused until the Blessed Virgin, his protectress since childhood, miraculously freed him. In this storm that finally made everyone lose courage, Holy Mother alone stood erect. Together with her daughters, she stormed heaven. She was indefatigable in encouraging her sons with letters and advice, in calling her friends for help, in presenting the true circumstances to the Father General who had once been so good to her, in appealing to her most powerful patron, the king, for protection. And finally she arrived at the solution that she recommended as the only possible one: the complete separation of the calced from the discalced Carmelites into two provinces. The Congregation of Religious in Rome had been occupied with the unfortunate conflict for a long time. A well-informed cardinal, whom Pope Gregory XIII questioned concerning the state of affairs, responded, "The Congregation has thoroughly investigated all the complaints of the Carmelites of the mitigated Rule. It comes down to the following: Those with the mitigated Rule fear that the reform will finally reform them also." The pope then decided that the monasteries of Carmelite friars and nuns of the reform were to constitute a province of their own under a provincial chosen by them. A brief dated June 27, 1580 announced this decision. In March of 1581, the chapter of Alcalá elected Fr. Jerónimo Gracián as its first provincial in accordance with the Holy Mother's wishes.

## 16. The End

Teresa greeted the end of the years of suffering with overflowing thanks. "God alone knew in full about the bitterness, and now only he alone knows of the boundless joy that fills my soul, as I see the end of these many torments. I wish the whole world would thank God with me! Now we are all at peace, calced and discalced Carmelites, and nothing is to stop us from serving God. Now then, my brothers and sisters, let us hurry to offer ourselves up for the honor of the divine Master who has heard our prayers so well" [F, 29, 31-32]. During the short span of time still given to her, she herself sacrificed her final strength for new journeys to make foundations. The erection of the monastery in Burgos, the last one that she brought to life, cost her much effort and time. She had left Avila on January 2, 1582, to go there. It was July before she could begin the trip home, but she was not to reach the desired goal any more. After she had visited a number of other monasteries of the nuns, Fr. Antonio of Jesus brought her to Alba to comply with a wish of the Duchess María Henríquez, the great patroness of that monastery. Completely exhausted, Teresa arrived on September 20. According to a number of witnesses, she had predicted some years earlier that she would die at this place and at this time. Even though the attending physician saw her condition as hopeless, she continued to take part in all the monastic exercises until September 29. Then she had to lie down. On October 2, in accordance with her wish, Fr. Antonio heard her last confession. On the third she requested Viaticum. An eyewitness gave this report: "At the moment when the Blessed Sacrament was brought into her cell, the Holy Mother raised herself without anyone's help and got on her knees. She would even have gotten out of her bed if she had not been prevented. Her expression was very beautiful and radiated divine love. With a lively expression of joy and piety, she spoke such exalted divine words to the Lord that we were all filled with great devotion." During the day she repeated again and again the words from the "Miserere" (Psalm 51): *Cor contritum et humiliatum, Deus, no despicies* ("A broken and contrite heart, God, you will not despise"). In the evening she asked to be anointed. Concerning her last day, October 4, we again have an eyewitness account by Sr. María of St. Francis:

> On the morning of the feast of St. Francis, at about 7 o'clock, our Holy Mother turned on her side toward the nuns, a crucifix in her hand, her expression more beautiful, more glowing, than I had ever seen it during her life. I do not know how her wrinkles disappeared, since the Holy Mother, in view of her great age and her continual suffering, had very deep ones. She remained in this position in prayer full of deep peace and great repose. Occasionally she gave some outward sign of surprise or amazement. But everything proceeded in great repose. It seemed as if she were hearing a voice that she answered. Her facial expression was so wondrously changed that it looked like a celestial body to us. Thus immersed in prayer, happy and smiling, she went out of this world into eternal life.

The wondrous events that occurred at the Saint's burial, the incorrupt state of her body that was determined by repeated disinterments, the numerous miracles that she worked during her life and then really in earnest after her death, the enthusiastic devotion of the entire Spanish people for their saint—all of this led to the initiation of the investigations preparatory to her canonization, already in the year 1595. Paul V declared her blessed in a brief on April 24, 1614. Her canonization by Gregory XV followed on March 22, 1622. Her feast day was designated as October 15, because the ten days after her death were dropped (October 5-14, 1582) due to the Gregorian calendar reform.

Luis de León[13] said of Teresa: "I neither saw nor knew the saint during her lifetime. But today, albeit she is in heaven, I know her and see her in her two living reflections, that is, in her daughters and in her writings...." Actually, there are few saints as humanly near to us as our Holy Mother. Her writings, which she penned as they came to her, in obedience to the order of her confessor, wedged in among all of her burdens and work, serve as classical masterpieces of Spanish literature. In incomparably clear, simple and sincere language they tell of the wonders of grace that God worked in a chosen soul. They tell of the indefatigable efforts of a woman with the daring and strength of a man, revealing natural intelligence and heavenly wisdom, a deep knowledge of human nature and a rich spirit's innate sense of humor, the infinite love of a heart tender as a bride's and kind as a mother's. The great family of religious[14] that she founded, all who have been given the enormous grace of being called her sons and daughters, look up with thankful love to their Holy Mother and have no other desire than to be filled by her spirit, to walk the way of perfection hand in hand with her to its goal.

Passport photo taken for Edith's transfer to the Carmel of Echt, Holland, in 1938, after the anti-Jewish violence of the *Kristallnacht.*

# II.3. St. Teresa Margaret of the Sacred Heart

On March 19, 1934, Pope Pius XI entered Blessed Teresa Margaret of the Sacred Heart in the register of saints. In Germany, the new saint is virtually unknown outside of our Order. Her life was quiet and hidden. She died on March 7, 1770 at the age of 22, and of this short lifespan, she spent five years in the Carmelite monastery in Florence. She performed no brilliant, attention-getting deeds, nor did her reputation reach the wider world. She was like a lily that, in a quiet vale protected from storms, rises slim and straight and, in the warm light of the sun, unfolds into a wondrous bloom. Her powerful and sweet fragrance charmed everyone who lived around her. Even after her death it did not evaporate, but spread wider and wider, and now it is to fill the entire church of God.

## 1. Childhood

Teresa Margaret is often compared with St. Aloysius. Like him, she not only died early, but also shared with him angelic purity and severe penance. Her home was Arezzo in Tuscany. Her parents, Ignatius Redi and Camilla Balleti, came from noble families. She was born on July 15, 1747, the eve of the feast of the Blessed Virgin Mary of Mount Carmel. She was baptized as Anna Maria. From early childhood on, she showed an unusual desire to hear people speak of God. When anyone talked of heavenly things in her presence, she fixed her eyes on the person's lips with such rapt attention that it had to amaze and move those present. When her confessor later asked her whether, from the moment she had gotten to know God she had also begun to love him, she replied, "But everyone does that, and how could anyone not do so?" This is how self-evident it was to her that one merely needed to know God in order to love him. Another time she said, "Jesus knows that from childhood on I never had any other wish than to please him and to become holy."

People often observed her even as a six-year-old gazing fixedly up to heaven for a long time as though in deep meditation. From her seventh year on she understood how to "find God in all things," in stars and flowers, in short, to read in all creatures a challenge to praise the Creator. When she was nine, her devout parents sent her to the Benedictine nuns at the monastery of St. Apollonia in Florence for her education.

67

She at once won the hearts of those in authority as well as her contemporaries by her exemplary zeal and obedience, by her natural lovableness, cheerfulness, and readiness to serve. With childish naïveté, she quite unconsciously expressed her continual union with God. "While we are enjoying ourselves, Jesus is thinking of us," she called to her playmates in the middle of recess. So it is understandable that people took unusual advantage of her reliability and would often entrust her with watching her companions, without this evoking any dissension.

When she saw the older pupils go to the communion rail, her behavior showed such a deep desire to be united with the Lord that she was given permission to receive her first Holy Communion at ten years of age—early for that time. She herself had not asked for it, for she was not in the habit of expressing wishes. Nor did she say anything about the result. But her increased faithfulness, her anxious avoidance of any shadow of sin, which often gave her sleepless nights for a presumed fault, bore persuasive witness.

Her rich interior life required discerning direction for her soul. Because she did not want to attract attention at the boarding school by staying in the confessional too long, she got the idea of confiding in her own father. In detailed letters she gave him an account of her spiritual life. She also asked him to destroy the letters at once. Since he did this conscientiously, none of this evidence has come down to us, except for the testimony of her father that they were full of the most exalted love of God and the most sensitive Christian perfection.

Probably at the suggestion of her father she also later consulted the confessor at the boarding school, Monsignor Pellegrini, and received from him direction in prayer and regulation of her penances, which she had already begun in her family home at an interior motivation.

A particular characteristic of her piety was her love of the Mother of God, which she harbored from early childhood. At the boarding school she once slipped on the steps while she was carrying a warming basin filled with glowing coals. She cried aloud to the Virgin Mary, whose picture hung near the foot of the stairs, and landed at the bottom completely unharmed; the coals had not even damaged her clothing.

Her constant spiritual recollection was evidenced by the calm, placid evenness of her disposition even though she was naturally high-spirited. And the fruit of her love for God was an untiring, loving readiness to serve everyone, not just the nuns and fellow boarders, but also the servants, from whom she liked to take over the heaviest tasks inconspicuously and as though for her own delight.

## 2. Religious Vocation

Anna Maria considered herself lucky to be living under the same roof with the Lord. With holy joy she participated in the monastery's routines. So it was only natural that the desire to spend her whole life in the house of the Lord should awaken in her. However, she still had no clarity about what order to choose. It was revealed to her in a singular way. She was 16 years old when one day in September of 1763 she was called into the speakroom with the nuns. It was a farewell visit of a childhood friend from her home town who was about to enter the Carmelite monastery of St. Teresa in Florence. On the way back inside the monastery, Anna Maria felt strangely uplifted and happy, and suddenly she heard a voice that spoke to her: "I am Teresa, and I want you to be one of my daughters." In doubt as to whether she should receive these words as divinely inspired, she rushed to the chapel to ask for complete clarity before the altar. Here that voice spoke for the second time and more clearly than before: "I am Teresa of Jesus, and I say to you that you will soon find yourself in my monastery."

Now complete calm settled over the soul of the young girl, and she decided to consecrate herself to God in Carmel. For the time being, she spoke with no one about this. And when shortly thereafter her father took her back to her family home, she kept her secret for several more months. She used this time to explore whether she would be equal to the strict lifestyle in Carmel. Without in the least neglecting her duties to her family, she remained in her room as much as possible to immerse herself in prayer and to read spiritual books. As much as consideration of her surroundings permitted, she practiced silence. She allowed no one to wait on her; in fact, when she could, she sought to do some of the servants' work. She let others choose her clothing without bringing up her own taste and, when possible, avoided changing her clothes during the day. She knew how to exercise secret mortifications during meals and to give to the poor some of what she denied herself. Indeed, she did not shrink from inflicting severe penances on her sensitive body.

After testing herself in this way for several months, it seemed to her time to take the steps necessary to carry out her decision. The first person in whom she confided was the Jesuit priest Jerome Maria Cioni. He advised her to discuss it with her mother. She chose her seventeenth birthday for this. Without her knowledge, her mother told her father. In spite of their piety, both parents were painfully disconcerted. However, it did not occur to them to refuse their consent outright. The only thing Count Redi deemed necessary was a thorough examination by experienced men of the spirit. Since everyone whose advice they sought definitely said that her vocation was genuine, Anna Maria received permission to write a letter to the mother superior of the Monastery of St. Teresa requesting admittance to the Order.

Objections raised by companions in her household and relatives could not dissuade the young candidate for the religious life in the least. Almost without meaning to, her father put her through a more difficult test. He and his favorite child had a habit of staying up together in the evenings to share their views on spiritual questions after the rest of the family had gone to bed. These hours gave both of them the greatest joy. One evening they were again sitting together. So far Count Redi had avoided discussing Anna Maria's plan with her. She did not even know that he was aware of it. On this evening he was suddenly overpowered by grief. He burst into tears and asked, "Do you really intend to leave me, my dear daughter?" Anna Maria loved her father tenderly. Not only was she bound to him by a child's natural attachments but, simultaneously, by a supernatural love for her spiritual director and confidant. Therefore, this surprising outburst must have touched her deeply. Count Redi himself described her behavior at that moment: "At this shock, probably the strongest possible to inflict on her sensitive heart under these circumstances, she remained standing motionless before me for a time as though animated by a higher spirit. Then she retreated to her room without saying a word."

When the answer from Florence came assuring Anna Maria's acceptance as a postulant, her father decided to take her to the monastery himself. Beforehand, at her mother's suggestion, one more special pleasure was afforded her: a pilgrimage to the nearby Mount Alvernia, to the holy place where St. Francis received the stigmata.

One day during the second half of August in the year 1764 Anna Maria left her home forever. Her mother was sick in bed. The departing daughter knelt before her to ask for her farewell blessing. Countess Redi could not say a single word; tears were all she had in reply. Anna Maria again remained very quiet and completely controlled her pain. After a few consoling words to his wife, Count Redi led her to the carriage. "After we had taken our places in it," he later said during the process, "without letting her know that I was observing her, I saw my daughter serious, motionless, and silent for a solid hour. Then her cheerful disposition returned, and she engaged me in merry and spirited conversation, continuing the journey in the most complete composure."

In Florence Anna Maria once more visited the nuns at St. Apollonia's who had raised her, to say good-bye to them and to her two younger sisters who were now pupils there. Then she stepped over the threshold of the Monastery of St. Teresa, which was now to become her home.

### 3. Life in the Order

The young sister used to call the convent that had admitted her the "house of angels." She considered all of her fellow sisters as angels. In her letter requesting admittance, she had said that her goal was to "compete with them in the holy love of God." She deemed belonging to this community an entirely undeserved grace and was continually grateful to the nuns. She was always convinced that she lived among them as someone entirely undeserving. With complete sincerity, she once said to her confessor, "Believe me, my Father, these nuns are saints and real angels. I tremble when I think of how different I am from them and how far from their example. Believe me, I am really unworthy to lay myself under their feet and to serve as a floor for them. By constantly giving them annoyance, all I am good for is to enable them to practice the virtue of patience continually. I do not know how they begin to tolerate me." At the same time, her behavior from the day of her entrance resembled that of a tried religious, so from that point of view there was never any doubt about her final acceptance after the probationary period.

But as the months of testing neared their end, another circumstance put the happy outcome in question: a virulent swelling above her right knee that would not go away for a long time. At first she tried to hide the trouble and knelt on the floor as always without support. But when she became feverish, the illness could no longer remain a secret. What gave her even more distress than the bodily pain was having to expose the affected part to the attending physician. She accepted the painful operation patiently in remembrance of the suffering Savior. Finally, the suffering abated and with it the impediment to her reception of the habit.

The sisters assembled in chapter to receive the postulant's request for acceptance. Fearful that she might be excluded because of her unworthiness, she knelt before the mother prioress and asked pardon for her failures, promising to do better. With great joy she heard the comforting assurance of the sisters who were completely convinced in their hearts of having obtained a consummate daughter of St. Teresa. But, in accord with the custom of that time, she had to wait two more months for the final vote and during this time even had to leave the enclosure. She spent the time in quiet withdrawal with Isabella Mozzi, a friend of her mother's in Florence.

March 11, 1765, was chosen for the clothing. On the eve, Anna Maria was permitted to return to the monastery. A large crowd of acquaintances and practically all the nobility of Florence were at the church where preparatory devotions were held to welcome her. They accompanied her to the door of the enclosure. Just as many participated at the clothing ceremony the following morning. At that time she received her religious name, *Teresa Margaret Marianne of the Sacred Heart of Jesus*.

The novice mistress into whose hands the young nun was entrusted, Teresa Maria Guadagni, had set as her goal the formation of her charges on the model of the oldest father of our Order, the strict hermit of Mount Carmel. The more she considered the perfection of which the new novice was capable and to which she was called, the sharper the

weapons she believed herself permitted to use to foster the practice and
to gain proficiency in the basic virtues of a religious: humility, obedience, self-abnegation. She knew how to find faults and shortcomings in
everything Margaret did and would reprimand her sharply. And when
the young sister acknowledged the correction by the customary prostra-
tion on the floor, the mistress was in no hurry at all to give her the signal
to rise. But no one ever saw a hint of bitterness or sensitivity in Margaret. However, when she was finally allowed to rise, she did so with a
friendly and cheerful expression and with the words, "God reward you
for your good deed."

Before her profession of vows, she had an experience of suffering
similar to that before her clothing. It was the same physical illness and,
after this had been healed successfully, there was the fear that they
would not allow her to make her profession because of her many faults
and imperfections. She could hardly believe it when the acceptance was
finally confirmed, and was full of gratitude for the undeserved grace.
She zealously examined herself to see whether she had any attachment
that might impede her complete union with the Lord. Her great love
for her father was the only thing that still caused her doubt. So she
decided to sacrifice the exchange of letters that she had been maintain-
ing up to then. She informed him that from now on they would meet in
the heart of Jesus and would see who could love God the most. When
incidentally another sister asked her, right after a visit from her father,
whether the farewell had not been difficult for her, she smiled and
showed her a scrap of paper on which some words of St. Augustine were
written: *Minus te amat, qui tecum aliquid amat.* "They love you too little
who continue to love anything other than you."

An eyewitness recounts of her profession on March 12, 1766: "At the
solemn moment of profession, she seemed to be transformed into a
seraph, and so deep and powerful was the impression of love her outward appearance made on the circle of sisters around her that they were
too moved and amazed to be able to restrain their tears."

The foundation of her life in the Order was her deep and living
faith. As during her childhood, so also later, she wanted to hear about
God and to enrich her knowledge. Even more than by books and priestly
instruction, this desire was satisfied by illumination from on high. Out
of this living faith arose a holy reverence for everything connected with
things of faith: for priests, for the other sisters as brides of Christ, for all
the altar vessels she cared for as sacristan, for all the rites during worship. Above all, the fruit of this living faith was constant living in God's
presence. Her confessor and spiritual director during her years in the
Order, Fr. Ildefonse, said during the process that in his judgment "her
prayer had reached the level of unity in faith where these kinds of souls
seem unable to continue to live much longer naturally. So in accord with
the usual way of God's providence, they tend to be called early into the

better world, there to see and to enjoy unveiled the Source of all being and all reality, the highest Lord whom they so eagerly sought to know on this miserable earth."

Her favorite expression was "God is love." And to requite this divine love with love in return was self-evident to her even from childhood. The thought of what the Lord suffered for us aroused in her the burning desire "to suffer a little for him, too." Therefore, she found no trial too hard; she discovered ever new sacrifices and penances. But she also knew that the Lord saw the proof of our love for him in the love we show to others. She found the occupation ideally suited for her love of neighbor in caring for the sick, when this responsibility was given to her after her profession. She was tireless in her care for those who were ill, and no impatience, no irritability or ingratitude of theirs could decrease her loving concern. Her strict superior, with whose care she was entrusted, knew how to try her most severely and had something to complain about in spite of all her eagerness. However, the caretaker always remained loving and patient. The ill mother prioress deliberately had to control herself so as not to express her wonder and gratitude for the tireless care. However, the only reason for this reticence was that she, too, considered it her duty to train her young daughter in humility and patience. In assuming the care of a mentally ill sister, the infirmarian took on a true martyrdom. But when they wanted to relieve her once more of this burden, she pleaded so hard to be allowed to continue to tend the patient that permission was granted her.

When the monastery was visited by an epidemic, her strength seemed to multiply. Indeed, it was apparent that supernatural gifts came to assist her in her duties. No matter how far away she was, she sensed when one of her patients needed her and was instantly at her side. A deaf elderly sister, with whom no one could communicate any longer, whom therefore even the confessor was no longer able to comfort, understood everything that Teresa Margaret said to her, even in a soft voice. So the infirmarian could care for her unhindered, and the patient also received from her the spiritual consolation for which she longed.

One day she found herself in the refectory with a sister who had been suffering from a severe toothache for a long time. Sr. Teresa Margaret saw that she was again in great pain. Full of sympathy, she arose, hurried over to the sufferer, and—in complete contrast to her former reserve the Constitutions of the Order also required—she pressed a kiss on the painful spot. Then she returned to her place. At that moment the pain left and did not return.

## 4. Death and Glorification

In the midst of these self-sacrificing deeds of love, she herself was called away. On March 4, 1770, she asked her confessor to allow her to make a general confession and to permit her to receive communion the next morning as though it were her last. Obviously, she had a premonition of her sudden death that would make it impossible for her to receive Viaticum. On the eve of March 6 she stayed to care for the sick so long that she could no longer have supper with the community. Somewhat later she went to the refectory to have the small collation served in Lent. There she was suddenly seized by severe pain resembling colic. She wanted to go to her cell, but could only drag herself as far as a room near the refectory. Only after a while, when the pain had abated enough, was she able to reach her cell. There she collapsed and had to call for help.

She was put to bed never to leave it again. For the whole night and the following day she was in unspeakable pain, but not for a moment did she lose patience; and every effort made on her behalf seemed to her to be too much. She would not allow a sister to watch beside her at night. Only under obedience did she permit a maid to remain with her. And all she requested of the maid was that she remain quiet so as not to disturb anyone's nightly rest. In the morning her first concern was that the young woman should make up the sleep she had missed. In the most severe pain, she gave the sisters instructions for the care of her patients. When she could no longer speak from pain, she turned her eyes to the cross that she was holding in her hand and pressed her lips to the wounds of the Crucified.

At about three o'clock in the afternoon, about the hour when our Lord died, she lost movement and speech. The confessor who was called could do nothing more than administer Extreme Unction to her. Soon thereafter she passed away quietly and peacefully.

Because of the illness that had carried her off, shortly after her death the corpse was very disfigured, the face and neck were blue and the body very swollen. The nuns were almost hesitant to place her on view at the grate in the church as was the custom. But even during the transfer, an amazing change began: The blue color changed to a delicate pallor, the face took on a rosy glow, the body turned slim and pliant. On March 9, the deceased seemed to be more beautiful and vibrant than when alive. Therefore, the Father Provincial permitted a postponement of the burial. Until March 22, that is, for fifteen days, the nuns kept their deceased sister in the church; not a trace of decomposition appeared. On that day the archbishop of Florence visited the corpse with many associates, including medical experts. Besides the miraculous preservation of the body, what attracted great crowds of the faithful—as at the death of our Holy Mother Teresa—was the unique fragrance that the corpse exuded. It spread to everything that came in contact with the deceased. Indeed, even the things that she had touched during life exuded it.

The holy body, which has remained incorrupt to this day, now rests in a glass shrine in the monastery church in Florence. Countless answers to prayers and cures of the sick led to early initiation of the beatification process so that her own father and confessor as well as a number of Carmelite nuns could make depositions.

In 1839, Pope Gregory XVI pronounced her virtues heroic. However, the beatification process was not concluded until the year 1929 under Pope Pius XI, and the jubilee of our salvation has now, on March 19, 1934, brought the canonization of the faithful follower of the Cross.

## II.4. A Chosen Vessel of Divine Wisdom:
### Sr. Marie-Aimée de Jésus
### of the Carmel of the Avenue de Saxe in Paris
### 1839-1874

"A page from the great book of God's mercy" is what Sister Marie-Aimée called her life. This life is very simple in its external course, but has an inner richness that can only be hinted at in a short biography. Those who would like to know more about it must refer to her own writings.[1]

### 1. Bethlehem

A delicate face of angelic purity and spirituality, big, soft, and deeply penetrating eyes that have knowledge of the supernatural world as well as of their natural home—this is Dorothea Quoniam, who in Carmel received the name of *Marie-Aimée de Jésus*. This name tells the secret of her life: "loved by Jesus" with an overwhelming, jealous love that laid total claim to her from her very first day. Her birthplace, a thatched hut in the Normandy village of Le Rozel, matches in poverty the stall in Bethlehem. A day laborer, her father works as a gardener, but is unable, even with all his diligence, to protect his own from the direst need. He is deeply religious and loves his wife and children with a tender and reverent love. Her mother had barely learned to read and write, but she is completely knowledgeable about the saints and raises her children with such heavenly wisdom that her daughter sees in her a likeness to the Blessed Virgin.

Dorothea is born on January 14. In the year of her birth, 1839, this day happened to be the feast of the Holy Name of Jesus. She was so weak at birth that emergency baptism had to be administered. Thereafter she recovered health and vitality. The name of Jesus was the first word that the lips of the child learned to form. Her mother's stories made her more at home in heaven than on earth. Inexhaustible were the mother's stories, insatiable the child's desire to hear. At four years of age, the little one hears from her mother's mouth the words: the *Almighty*. They captivate her. As usual, she wants to withdraw to a lonely place to reflect on what she has heard. But she is held fast at the threshold of the hut as if by an invisible force. Raising her eyes to heaven, she constantly repeats interiorly "the Almighty." Then she looks at herself and says, "How little I am!" She herself recounts:

> And suddenly the Spirit of my dearly Beloved raised me to the incorruptible heights, not only once, but several times, all the way to the Almighty, the *one* God in three Persons. The Holy Spirit, like an eagle mother, held me, this little eagle child, in the claws of its love, so that I could stand the intense glow of the Sun of Righteousness and remain in the presence of the Father in whom the Son appeared to me; so that I was able to bear the excess of happiness and splendor, as I learned that I was destined to become the bride of my Lord—me, a poor, fragile creature—if I consented. I consented and became engaged to my Beloved.[2]

This was not the dream of an active imagination. It was the decisive event of her life. From then on, she saw herself as the bride of the Lord, as God's exclusive property. She was soon to discover that she was engaged to the Crucified. Even in these tender years of childhood a chain of suffering began that would not end until her death. Necessity forced her father to move his entire family to Paris in compliance with his brother's kind offer to help support them more effectively there. Instead of the open countryside, her home is now an attic on the eighth floor of an apartment building. They took off Dorothea's country garb and made her into a little Parisienne. The child's sensitive heart suffered greatly. But the others adjusted without complaining. So she bore her pain silently, too. Soon there were to come even more severe tests. Yet the best thing she possessed went with her: Jesus, who speaks to her in her heart, and her mother in whom she senses the presence of the Lord himself. She is the confidante of her interior life. Yet there are some things, especially the most acute suffering, that no one knows but the heavenly Bridegroom. The child already knows how to keep the secret of the King, and the mother is in awe of this. She guesses much without it being said. The treasure with which heaven has entrusted her is completely clear to her. She does her best to support the work of grace in this elect soul.

Soon an early apostolate begins. At six years of age Dorothea was entrusted as a day pupil to the Sisters of Charity (Vincentians) at St. Roch's parish. The richness of her interior life insists on being communicated. During free time she knows how to talk about Jesus and Mary in a charming way. Her little companions gather around her and never tire of listening to her. She also has other friends whom she tries to win for God. When Mrs. Quoniam goes down the street with her little daughter, she notices that all kinds of people, big and small, greet the child

with marks of love and respect. These are the poor people to whom she
has given left-over morsels and has at the same time fed on heavenly
doctrine. A burning zeal for God's honor fills the little bride of God. She
carefully watches the behavior of the people, is happy when they honor
the Lord, full of pain when they do not. A sense of dread fills her when
she encounters people who live in sin. A burning desire to go into the
wilderness or to suffer martyrdom grips her. Yet soon she has something
else to wish for as well. She hears that the Mother of God died of love.
This she wants, too, and she will never not stop asking to die of love.

Anyone zealous for God's honor will inevitably summon an embit-
tered adversary to the arena: the enemy of all goodness from the beginning. He inflicts on Dorothea nocturnal fears and bodily assaults. He
tries to get her to blaspheme God. She suffers unspeakably, but remains
faithful. Added to these and other interior sufferings is the bitter poverty. The family no longer has the basic necessities. It must accept the
help of good-hearted friends and public assistance. The hands of the
child that so enjoyed giving gifts must open to receive them. The bride
of the humble Savior learns to bear all kinds of humiliation. But all the
support is insufficient. Parents and siblings are ravaged by their destitu-
tion. Two little siblings die soon after birth.[3] An older brother, a child of
grace like Dorothea, pined away and died the death of a saint. The
mother drags on as long as she possibly can. But she senses that the end
is near. She teaches the child to carry out all the tasks of the little household, shows her how to do what is necessary. Dorothea is nine and one-
half years old when she leaves school to oversee the household and care
for her mother. Finally, her father also has to stop working. The physician says that the child will certainly collapse under the weight of caring
for both of them. After a heartbreaking farewell, the fatally ill man is
taken to a hospital. Mother and child are bound together most intimately during these days of illness. An interior pronouncement gives
Dorothea certainty of the imminent death of the people she loves the
most. She proposes that her mother receive the last sacraments and with
her consent makes all the arrangements. During the celebration, the
relatives are torn with pain, but the sick woman is filled with heavenly
bliss. As the end draws near, she has the good relatives who had done so
much for the family summoned. It is late in the evening. Aunt and uncle
lovingly insist that the exhausted little one go to bed. The mother makes
this last sacrifice. Nor will she allow the child to be awakened when the
last moment comes. All she does is to raise herself once more with her
last strength to look over to the other bed. Dorothea is always convinced
that her mother blessed her in this last moment as she had promised
earlier. When the child awakens, the mother has been dead for an hour.
It is the morning of January 9, 1850.

Here ends the story of her childhood. It gives off the gentle fragrance of medieval legends. The recounting of the death of her mother is reminiscent of one of the loveliest poems of German romanticism: the story of beautiful Els of Laurenburg in Clemens Brentano's "Chronika eines fahrenden Schülers" [*Chronicles of an Itinerant Scholar*]. However, here is no legend or poem, but actual events full of fruitful seeds for the future.

## 2. Nazareth

The devoted relatives and a number of family friends would gladly have adopted the lovable child. However, her mother had decided something else. According to her wish, the child was to be raised in the orphanage of the Sisters of Charity, protected by the sanctuary from the dangers of the world. Dorothea was not placed with her former teachers at St. Roch's Parish, but into a different house designated for children who were not very well and needed care. This was another wound to her loving heart. Four weeks later her father died and soon thereafter her little sister. Her oldest brother, who was still alive, had already caused his mother much concern. He was very talented and won all hearts, but in a secular environment lost his own faith. When he became fatally ill at the age of eighteen, his sister feared for his eternal salvation. Her prayers and her loving influence led to his reconciliation with God. During his last days he no longer wanted to see anyone except a priest and her, whom he called his angel. When he closed his eyes, her last earthly tie was severed. Jesus had taken everything from his bride; she was to find her entire happiness in him, and the graces he poured over her in her quiet "Nazareth" were superabundant. On September 8, 1851, she had the joy, so long desired, of receiving her first Holy Communion. She was like the deer that has found water, like a child in the arms of its mother. Even twenty years later her companions recalled her angelic recollection, her seraphic devotion on Communion days. In no way could the working of grace in this elect creature remain hidden from those around her, even though no one was initiated into the secrets of her interior life.

Probably she was subject to occasional enmity and misunderstanding, but her imperturbable gentleness and goodness overcame all obstacles. She had a most beneficial influence on her companions, for which the nuns could not give enough thanks. In all secrecy, the Lord himself formed her soul. Unnoticed by those watchful of her, she practiced the most severe acts of self-denial, so that all the loving concern for her fragile health was to no avail. By tender reproaches and finally by forbidding her Communion, the Savior led her back from a short time of vanity and distraction. Then when he again invited her to the eucharistic meal, he took possession of her heart anew and locked it forever against everything other than himself. Occasionally, he revealed himself to her in human form and each time corresponding to her age, so that he seemed to grow up with her. When she was nineteen, her relatives wanted to arrange her future. One day they introduced a young man to her, and, after an opening conversation, let her know that he came as a suitor. Dorothea said not a word. She only smiled, but this smile was of a kind that made the poor fellow lower his eyes, blush, and wish that he had never come. The Lord had revealed himself beside this young man "in the full radiance of his virginal beauty" and said, "Compare!" At the same time, a smile of divine irony played about his lips and evoked its reflection in the face of his bride. The first attempt of this kind was rejected, and she knew how to refuse all thereafter with calm firmness. She had already known when she moved to her "Nazareth" that her aim was the "desert" of Carmel. But she had to await the Lord's hour.

In 1857 it appeared as though her hopes could soon be fulfilled. It had turned out to be very inconvenient for the orphans to be separated in two homes in different parts of the city. Therefore, it was decided to combine them and house them in another building. On this occasion, most of the sisters were transferred and many pupils left. It was a large, painful break-up. Dorothea's relatives now wanted to take her with them, too; and she hoped this would make it easier for her to gain admittance to the Order. Then she was asked to move into the new house. It was expected that merging both groups of pupils would involve great difficulties. Dorothea was to be an angel of peace in bridging the differences. She consented and silently made the sacrifice of seeing the fulfillment of her longing postponed indefinitely. The superior, Sr. Eugénie Michelin, received her with love and gratitude. She had heard many good things about the young lady, but soon saw even her expectations surpassed. Dorothea worked under the direction of the saintly young Sr. Louise Rousseille. Both were soon united in heart and soul. However, Sr. Louise died just one year later. Her young companion had to finish the work of reconciliation alone. Here, too, the irresistible influence of her personality succeeded, and even more, perhaps, her prayer and suffering.

Up to then she was unacquainted with any mystical writings. Nor was she conscious of the extraordinary graces she had received. She assumed that such things happened to everyone. Since no one spoke of them, she thought this was something that was supposed to be kept secret, and was herself silent, even in the confessional. Then a biography of Holy Mother Teresa came into her hands. The saint's concern over deception aroused in her the fear of being prey to the Prince of Lies. But Holy Mother [Teresa] also showed her where to find help: talking with an enlightened man of the spirit. She began to plead constantly that a qualified priest be sent to her. Her prayer was heard when an experienced religious priest came to hold a retreat for the pupils. Dorothea opened herself to him and was completely freed of her fears, and also strengthened in her vocation to Carmel.

## 3. The Desert

Dorothea's call to Carmel had already occurred when she was a child. Once when she began to take pleasure in frivolous things and endanger her interior life, her mother gave her a book that contained a short biography of Holy Mother Teresa. She found herself reflected in it word for word. "This child, upon whom God had bestowed so many graces, who loved good books and religious conversations, so longed for martyrdom, and, since she could not have this, placed her hope in the life of a hermit—was that not I?"[4] But she also saw her own image in Teresa's involvement with frivolous friends and the consequent cooling of her ardor. Teresa finds herself again during her education in a monastery—"I am that child from this moment on. Teresa is steadfast in doing good and consecrates herself to Jesus in the Order of Our Lady of Mount Carmel. This is the way opening before me. This is my way to heaven.... Teresa lives and dies holy. I also want to live and die holy."

Dorothea confided her decision to her mother at that time and found delighted agreement. She never wavered in it. After the long years of waiting, the fulfillment now seemed near, since her task in the orphanage was finished. The grateful superiors wanted to place no further hindrance in the path of the beloved child. But now difficulties from another side arose. Originally, Dorothea had thought only of the first Parisian Carmel. It was the only one she knew. It was near the orphanage on West Street and was often visited by the sisters with their pupils. But on a longer walk one day, they turned in at the Carmel on the Avenue de Saxe. Upon stepping over the threshold, the future Carmelite perceived—she was then about seventeen years old—these words within her: "This is where I want you." The impression was so strong that she asked her superior for permission to call on the prioress of this Carmel. She was received with friendliness and encouraged to return. But her youth, her fragile health, and lack of means aroused the concern of the older sisters so that her admission was delayed for a long time. It was suggested that she choose another order. But that was out of the question for her. "I need Carmel...with its perfection and way of perfection, Carmel with its purity, its apostolate, its martyrdom; Carmel with its special love for the sacred humanity of our Lord and its veneration of the Blessed Virgin without being restricted to one of her states or mysteries."[5]

She had tried to get to know the main orders thoroughly.

Each has its letter and its spirit, but I want the one that unites a rigorous letter with the spirit of love. Each has its goal, but I want the goal of supporting the church and converting sinners. Each has its principal means, but I want that of prayer. Each has its advantages, but I want that of solitude. Each has its fame, but I humbly pass by the one famed for its learning, reverently bow before the one known for its silence. I strike my breast when I pass the one famed for its penance, am enthusiastic about the one known for its poverty. However, I rush toward the one that has above all glories the incomparable glory of love....[6]

Nor could Dorothea consider any other Carmel than the one that seemed to be stubbornly closed to her. God's will was too clear to her. And her trust was finally rewarded. A newly elected prioress, Mother Sophie of St. Elijah, remembered her and invited her anew. Her faithful maternal protector, the superior, Sr. Eugénie Michelin, became her indefatigable ally. The latter's intelligence finally triumphed over the opposition of Dorothea's all-too-loving uncle and thereby secured a small dowry. On August 27, 1859, the feast of the Transverberation of the Heart of Holy Mother Teresa, she was permitted to escort her ward into Carmel. It was at exactly the time that the Lord had given to his faithful bride a year earlier.

The house that accepted the young postulant had an excellent spirit. Most of the sisters had been formed by the valiant foundress, Camille of the Child of Jesus [de Soyecourt]. Mother Sophie was a true mother, as good as she was firm, full of understanding and with a reverence for extraordinary graces, even though she herself was not led on this path. The novice mistress, Isabelle of the Nativity, was an exemplary religious, but her exaggerated fearfulness prevented her from reaching this extraordinary soul. Dorothea could not be open with her, and soon even had to bear the novice mistress's giving credence to malicious slander [against Dorothea]. Her interior life, her intimate relationship with the Lord, remained completely hidden from everyone. He placed only one director at her side with whom she could be open about everything without reserve. This director too, had already been promised her before her entrance. He was the extraordinary confessor to the monastery, Fr. Gamard, S.J. He was clear very soon about the specially graced child that was being entrusted to him, and stood faithfully by her side through all the trials of her thorny ascent.

Life in the monastery suited her deepest inclinations, especially the seven hours of service in the choir every day, the solitude, and the silence. Another sister once saw her standing listening in her cell with the door open during the midday silence. Later she asked her what she had been doing there. She answered that she had been listening to the silence. She wrote down for this sister what it had told her. So originated the wonderfully deep little paper about the twelve levels of silence.[7] Before her clothing, concern was again raised about her fragile health. But she finally received admission anyway. At the celebration on February 15, 1860, the respect that this young orphan enjoyed in the widest circles became evident. Not only did the faithful sisters and companions from the orphanage participate, but also people of every standing who had come to know her there. The happy bride would gladly have had the whole world participate for the greater honor of her divine bridegroom.

A harder battle ensued over her admission to profession. The time of testing was lengthened to include Lent of the year 1861. The idea was to see if her health was up to this ordeal. During these weeks, constant visions of suffering consumed her strength, without anyone except Fr. Gamard knowing anything about them. While the sisters were gathered in chapter, Marie-Aimée saw her mother pleading before the throne of the Most Blessed Trinity for mercy for her child. The decision was obviously on the turn of a blade. The endangered one gathered all her strength and united her prayer with that of her faithful advocate. A moment later her mother turned to her with a radiant smile. Then the vision vanished. The novice mistress came and brought the news that she had been admitted.

The celebration was set for April 18. For the ten-day preparatory retreat, the theme of a Carmelite's day was set for her. The mistress had no idea of the illuminations that the Holy Spirit would grant to her novice while meditating on this intentionally sober and simple material. On April 10, Jesus showed her his soul in its heavenly beauty in an intellectual vision. On the morning of the day of the profession, he himself instructed her in how he wanted to be loved by her. As the result of this teaching, Marie-Aimée wrote down the following solemn explanation: "Not for all the world do I want the wife of a mortal person to serve me as a model or even surpass me in the love that I must cherish for my Lord Jesus Christ, nor in the demonstrations of love that I owe him. I will be adamant with all of them over this."[8] At the moment when she took the vows, her physical surroundings vanished before her eyes; she saw the Most Holy Trinity and saw the Son of God bending down to her and taking her as his bride.

Even though those around her were not told about what was going on within the young Carmelite, the consequences of such fullness of grace could not remain hidden. Her entire nature breathed God's presence. Her life in the Order was formed by the Holy Spirit down to the most insignificant external activities. She was inexhaustible in demonstrating sisterly love, especially when there was a chance of inflaming hearts to a greater love of God. So she could not help but win everyone over. But this did not prevent a difficult trial from befalling her even during the first year of her profession. With the permission of the mother prioress, a young nun had come to her for help on the path to perfection. The frequent conversations brought both of them under suspicion of an inappropriate attraction (for this, also, the Lord had prepared his bride before her entrance into the Order) and led to their being watched constantly, so that they finally had to give up all contact. Great bodily suffering was soon added; this excluded the zealous religious from the beloved community exercises and also kept her from doing external penances. More terrible than all this were the spiritual nights, times of the utmost darkness and abandonment. But nothing could quench the thirst for suffering of the faithful bride of Christ. She wanted to go the entire way of the Cross with her Lord. The fruit of all these trials was an ever more intimate union, an ever increasing growth into the likeness of Jesus.

## 4. The Task

In the desert solitude the instrument was forged, hardened in the fire of suffering. It lay ready for action in the hand of the Master. And the Lord did not hesitate to make use of it.

In the year 1863 there appeared the *Life of Jesus* by Renan. During recreation, Mother Sophie spoke to her daughters of the devastating impact of this book in order to invite their reparation. A number of sisters could not help looking at Sister Marie-Aimée. Her work dropped from her hands, her face became white as a sheet, she began to tremble. She seemed close to fainting. Everyone knew of her fervent love of God. So they understood that her pain must be particularly great. But no one could really fathom what was actually happening in her. From the first days of her life, the Lord had taken possession of her. Jesus Christ, in his divinity and humanity, was the Life of her life, the truest reality that she knew. She saw the divine Bridegroom at her side as she walked through the cloister halls. He awaited her in her cell when she returned to her cherished solitude after obligatory work. He sat at her left side in the empty choir stall during the Divine Office. Now a "new Arius" dared to deny the divinity of Jesus, to stamp him as an ordinary person. Could there be a greater insult? "All for the greater honor of God" was the motto of her life. Now this honor was at stake. In her solitary cell she shed a stream of tears. She felt compelled to undertake some kind of defense. "How," she cried out, "if I am the bride, can I keep silent? ...I cannot speak..., well then, I will write!" She recalled how Moses raised his hands to heaven on the mountain and prayed while the Israelites battled in the valley. But to pray, to suffer, and to weep were not enough for her while bishops and priests engaged in the open battle. "Yes, I will remain on the mountain, but from this peak I will call down, 'Jesus is the Son of God!' Yes, I will pray, suffer, shed tears; but after I have prayed, I will write with my blood and my tears, 'Jesus is the Son of God!'"

She picked up a pen and wrote on a little piece of paper, "In the beginning was the Word, and the Word was with God, and God was the Word." Then a spirit seized her that was not her own, light streamed over her, words formed themselves. In a few moments the paper was covered. She had begun to prove the divinity of Jesus Christ with the words of the holy Scriptures.[9] After a while she paused, frightened. She wanted to burn what she had written, but she could not.

When she told Fr. Gamard about her wish to do battle with Renan, he expressed his astonishment, for he knew that she had no background at all for such an undertaking. She handed him a notebook in which she had written from memory some clarifications on certain questions of the interior life that he had given to her eight days earlier. He himself says about this, "In her writing my thoughts were raised to such heights, my modest speech so transformed, the doctrine presented with such complete exactness, that reading it was like a revelation for me."[10] Thereafter he was willing to assume that the desire to respond to Renan also came from the Holy Spirit. But before he could tell Marie-Aimée to write, she informed him that she had already started and told him what happened when she did so. She said that not only did overwhelming light flood her, but that also her hand was unusually facile and that it was impossible for her to burn the pages. He told her that in no way must she do so, and forbade her any further efforts. He expressed his willingness to examine the beginnings of her work. She herself was to obtain the permission of the mother prioress for this and was to inform her about what she had already done. Since an examination of the writing aroused great hopes, the young Carmelite received the charge to continue with the work from both Fr. Gamard and the mother prioress. But no one in the house was to know anything about it. Thus, the only time granted her for this was the sisters' free time. For a long while she had only one hour a day available to work. To this were added all sorts of other difficulties and distress that should naturally have thwarted success. There were continual new bodily illnesses, interior doubt and disturbances, a lack of understanding by those around her. The burden was increased when Mother Isabelle was elected prioress. She now had to be let in on the secret and give her consent. Fearful as she was, Mother Isabelle did not dare to interrupt a task that had been sanctioned by her predecessor and a highly respected theologian. But she was in constant fear that the young sister could be the victim of a delusion and repeatedly raised new doubts in the already anxious sister. And then Fr. Gamard was called back to Paris and could now only give advice, comfort, and reassurance in infrequent letters. But no hindrance could put a stop to the work that God himself had initiated and commanded.

Marie-Aimée did not give herself a moment's rest. As soon as the time allowed came, she set to work even if she was dead tired and plagued by pain. And as soon as she picked up her pen, the Spirit came over her. The Lord himself instructed her. He did not want her to consult intellectual works. Without her making any kind of plan, a clear structure appeared that became evident to her only afterward. The first part treated of the Eternal Word in the bosom of the Father and the Incarnate Word in the womb of Mary; the second about the hidden life of Jesus; the third about his public ministry; the fourth and last about his suffering, his death, and his life in glory. A great many scriptural passages from the Old and New Testaments came to her whenever she needed them. They came to her with their references. Subsequent checks confirmed them to be accurate. Everything was of the greatest theological clarity, sharpness, and exactness. It was the pure doctrine of the church, but written in the language of love. Accordingly, every observation included a presentation of how this mystery affected the loving soul. These comments offered excellent pointers for the interior life. The Lord set special importance on them.

On July 4, 1865, Marie-Aimée could announce to Fr. Gamard the conclusion of the last part. He found in it very little requiring substantial correction. But its external form appeared to him to require a second revision. The young Carmelite promptly set to it, but after a while her spiritual director himself called for a break. He commissioned her to write an account of the graces God had shown to her. In her hands this report became the story of her life. (Her letters to Fr. Gamard are an adjunct to it, since after his transfer she had to communicate with him in writing.) Thereafter, she was permitted to return to her main work. But even now there was no lack of severe interior and outer trials. A new superior, Abbé le Rebours, had to be let in on the secret and be asked for permission for the work to continue. He granted it and was soon entirely won over to the gifted young religious, but first she had to undergo a painful test. The most thorough study of the Gospels was the basis for the second revision of her work. But this time also the Lord did what was most essential for its success. He initiated his faithful disciple in all the mysteries of his life and suffering by actually letting her experience with him what she was to present. Occasionally, this involved suffering that would have overwhelmed her delicate nature had she not had the extraordinary support of grace to preserve her life for her task. She was only permitted to present Jesus' eucharistic life very briefly, because this life itself and the participation in it of the soul conformed to God is a hidden life.

After five years of devoted labor, the work was concluded on the feast of Holy Mother Teresa on October 15, 1869. Now Marie-Aimée was permitted to spend the rest of her life entirely with Christ in God in accordance with her deepest inclination. Her public task was fulfilled. Her superiors and the sisters would gladly have had her clarify some things. But she was not to write any more. She even destroyed voluminous notes on the Song of Songs to protect herself from being misunderstood. Nevertheless, many of her thoughts had already been taken up by people who, through misunderstanding them, drew false conclusions and occasioned new attacks.

Since Marie-Aimée had lived "from hand to mouth" when she first wrote her work, her goal as well as its structure had not become completely clear until she had reworked the manuscript. In every chapter the first part is devoted to the demonstration of Christ's divinity. The second is intended to "lead the soul to imitate Jesus Christ; to commandeer her at the beginning after she has decided to take the path to perfection, and then to lead her to the peak of perfection on the path of pure love by persistent elaboration and simplification," to make "of her a victim of love...."[11]

What Sister Marie-Aimée was trying to do by these teachings on the interior life was also the fruit of her life itself. From childhood on, she had been an apostle of divine love: with her fellow students, with the pupils at the orphanage, and finally with the other nuns. She witnessed the consummation of Sr. Aloysia Gonzaga. The bond of these two souls had aroused so much disturbance in the monastery and caused them both much suffering and humiliation, but it was desired by the Lord. He illumined his favored bride so that she could help her sister to ascend, gave her the consolation of seeing her die a holy death, and permitted her to effect a quick passage from the place of purification into heavenly glory.

During the war of 1870-1871, she was the support of the house by her quiet trust and her imperturbable interior peace. At her suggestion, the monastic family secured the special protection of heaven through a vow, and remained completely intact during the bombardment.

During the last years of her life (1871-1874), she was also entrusted with the formation of the novices. She undertook and carried out her duties in deepest humility, trusting in Jesus alone. Her example itself was powerful in forming souls; her obvious union with God must have been attractive. But she was also an energetic guide. When necessary, she did not shrink from severe, decisive actions. But even then it was clearly evident that she did so out of love, a truly divine love that enveloped the entrusted souls with tireless care. In addition, she possessed supernatural illumination that disclosed the souls to her and let her know exactly what they required, what circumstances they would meet, and how they needed to be prepared for these. One of the novices had already been recommended to her by the Lord when the novice was still a child of twelve years and Marie-Aimée eighteen. Both were still far from Carmel at that time and unknown to each other. But when the postulant presented herself in the speakroom, the young mistress of novices recognized her as one of the souls especially entrusted to her. Soon after the death of her mistress, this novice recorded her impressions, "I saw Sr. Aimée de Jésus for the first time in May of 1871 at the time when I wished to enter Carmel. My impression when the grille was opened was one of deep gratitude to the Lord who had...heard my plea to give me a *saint* to introduce me to the religious life. The expression on her so completely quiet and pure face, her all-penetrating look, immediately convinced me that she read my soul profoundly, to its depths...." At first a certain shyness kept her from expressing herself verbally. Therefore, she decided to open her heart in writing. "She came to me, looked at me gently, and said a few words. That was all, but how much this look taught me! ...(I had) the innermost conviction that my soul was joined to hers, that a saint was taking me as her child, that in her and through her Jesus would now and in the future give himself to his little creature...."

### 5. *Consummatum est* ["It Is Finished"]

While Marie-Aimée was forming young souls for her beloved Lord, he himself completed his work in her soul. Her union with the Incarnate God and the entire Blessed Trinity became ever deeper and ever more complete, the release from everything earthly. Trials and sufferings of all kinds accompanied all this. Illness and weakness became more and more prevalent. Rumors that spread about the work of the simple Carmelite led to attacks by priestly circles so that finally the judgment of the papal nuncio had to be solicited. The superior, who had appeared so gracious at first, repeatedly initiated strong opposition to her. By his interference he even, for a time, brought things to the point of clouding the understanding she had with her faithful director. Moreover, when she was dying, he put her to a test that greatly dismayed all the sisters. He had offered to administer Extreme Unction to her himself. After she had asked the assembled community for forgiveness as was customary, he commanded her also to ask for forgiveness for the aggravation (scandal) that she had caused. She repeated the words he enunciated for her in complete calm. The distress of the sisters was all the greater because during her last illness even her strongest opponents had become convinced of her holiness. She caught the flu at the beginning of January, 1874, soon after her last retreat. It happened that she was nursed by sisters who earlier had been very much against her. They surrounded her with nothing but love and saw it as a grace to be allowed to do so. Twice they observed that her head was surrounded by light for an extended time and that her expression then resembled that of a three- or four-year-old child.

At this time Mother Isabelle, the former novice mistress, was again prioress. She, too, was now certain of the treasure the house possessed in this invalid. She also felt very much responsible for her work and even directed Marie-Aimée to arrange and edit her handwritten papers on her deathbed. After that distressing incident when Extreme Unction was given, Mother Isabelle asked the superior the reason for his actions. "I wanted to give an example," he said, "and to show what virtue can do. I myself also wanted to be certain of the kind of spirit that had been leading this nun during her life." Thereafter the prioress went to the patient and urgently asked her about her spiritual disposition. As an answer Marie-Aimée gave her a piece of paper that bore her writing in pencil and said, "My soul has been in this disposition since my last retreat and during this illness." She had written in the third person, but it was an account of her own spiritual state intended for Fr. Gamard:

> This soul forgets everything; she is like an alien. She no longer petitions for herself, but the Holy Spirit inspires her with prayers that completely correspond to her requirements and are of great perfection.... This soul is at peace. For the most part, she does not dwell on the graces she used to receive and cannot even do so.... If she must write about them, she does so immediately and limits herself to important aspects that especially occur to her and whose communication she sees will serve the glory of God or the salvation of souls.... This soul no longer considers herself superior to others and judges nothing. She disdains herself and esteems others very highly.... She no longer knows hypocrisy, but is as simple as a child.... She desires for herself and in everything only the fulfillment of what pleases God. She desires no more talent, graces, or holiness than God has decided to give to her. Indeed she has an unquenchable thirst for suffering and humiliation, but still she wants only what God wants.... She turns naturally to Jesus as if he alone existed. And since he always answers her, she forgets more and more all that is created and depends on her dearly beloved alone. She is free, nothing disconcerts her. She is ready to obey anyone.... Looking at her failures does not disconcert her, and she seldom notices those of others and always forgives them.

During her last days, her increasing desire for the vision of God, the longing to die of love, was in conflict with her wish to suffer. Having gone the entire way of the cross with the Lord, she now had to share with him the ultimate, abandonment by God. Then came the peace of eternity. On May 4, 1874, about 9 o'clock in the morning, she raised "her eyes to heaven, smiled with an expression of mingled happiness, surprise, and delight, raised herself up as if to soar aloft to him whom she had loved so much, and expired so that no one could perceive her last breath."[12] What she had once rejoiced about in a hymn of thanks to the Lord was accomplished: "My dearly beloved has taken me from myself to become more his own! I am the prey of his love! He is in me like a fiery torrent, sweeping my soul into the sea of endless love, into God."

The Carmel of Echt, Holland, where Edith arrived on December 31, 1938.

# III

## At the Foot of the Cross

### III.1. Love of the Cross: Some Thoughts for the Feast of St. John of the Cross

We hear repeatedly that St. John of the Cross desired nothing for himself but to suffer and be despised. We want to know the reason for this love of suffering. Is it merely the loving remembrance of the path of suffering of our Lord on earth, a tender impulse to be humanly close to him by a life resembling his? This does not seem to correspond to the lofty and strict spirituality of the mystical teacher. And in relation to the Man of Sorrows, it would almost seem that the victoriously enthroned king, the divine conqueror of sin, death, and hell is forgotten. Did not Christ lead captivity captive? Has he not transported us into a kingdom of light and called us to be happy children of our heavenly Father?

The sight of the world in which we live, the need and misery, and the abyss of human malice, again and again dampens jubilation over the victory of light. The world is still deluged by mire, and still only a small flock has escaped from it to the highest mountain peaks. The battle between Christ and the Antichrist is not yet over. The followers of Christ have their place in this battle, and their chief weapon is the cross.

What does this mean? The burden of the cross that Christ assumed is that of corrupted human nature, with all its consequences in sin and suffering to which fallen humanity is subject. The meaning of the way of the cross is to carry this burden out of the world. The restoration of freed humanity to the heart of the heavenly Father, taking on the status of a child, is the free gift of grace, of merciful love. But this may not occur at the expense of divine holiness and justice. The entire sum of human failures from the first Fall up to the Day of Judgment must be blotted out by a corresponding measure of expiation. The way of the cross is this

91

expiation. The triple collapse under the burden of the cross corresponds to the triple fall of humanity: the first sin, the rejection of the Savior by his chosen people, the falling away of those who bear the name of Christian.

The Savior is not alone on the way of the cross. Not only are there adversaries around him who oppress him, but also people who succor him. The archetype of followers of the cross for all time is the Mother of God. Typical of those who submit to the suffering inflicted on them and experience his blessing by bearing it is Simon of Cyrene. Representative of those who love him and yearn to serve the Lord is Veronica. Everyone who, in the course of time, has borne an onerous destiny in remembrance of the suffering Savior or who has freely taken up works of expiation has by doing so canceled some of the mighty load of human sin and has helped the Lord carry his burden. Or rather, Christ the head effects expiation in these members of his Mystical Body who put themselves, body and soul, at his disposal for carrying out his work of salvation. We can assume that the prospect of the faithful who would follow him on his way of the cross strengthened the Savior during his night on the Mount of Olives. And the strength of these crossbearers helps him after each of his falls. The righteous under the Old Covenant accompany him on the stretch of the way from the first to the second collapse. The disciples, both men and women, who surrounded him during his earthly life, assist him on the second stretch. The lovers of the cross whom he has awakened and will always continue to awaken anew in the changeable history of the struggling church, these are his allies at the end of time. We, too, are called for that purpose.

Thus, when someone desires to suffer, it is not merely a pious reminder of the suffering of the Lord. Voluntary expiatory suffering is what truly and really unites one to the Lord intimately. When it arises, it comes from an already existing relationship with Christ. For, by nature, a person flees from suffering. And the mania for suffering caused by a perverse lust for pain differs completely from the desire to suffer in expiation. Such lust is not a spiritual striving, but a sensory longing no better than other sensory desires, in fact worse, because it is contrary to nature. Only someone whose spiritual eyes have been opened to the supernatural correlations of worldly events can desire suffering in expiation, and this is only possible for people in whom the spirit of Christ dwells, who as members [*Glieder*][1] are given life by the Head, receive his power, his meaning, and his direction. Conversely, works of expiation bind one closer to Christ, as every community that works together on one task becomes more and more closely knit and as the limbs [*Glieder*] of a body, working together organically, continually become more strongly one.

But because *being* one with Christ is our sanctity, and progressively *becoming* one with him our happiness on earth, the love of the cross in no way contradicts being a joyful child of God. Helping Christ carry his cross fills one with a strong and pure joy, and those who may and can do so, the builders of God's kingdom, are the most authentic children of God. And so those who have a predilection for the way of the cross by no means deny that Good Friday is past and that the work of salvation has been accomplished. Only those who are saved, only children of grace, can in fact be bearers of Christ's cross. Only in union with the divine Head does human suffering take on expiatory power. To suffer and to be happy although suffering, to have one's feet on the earth, to walk on the dirty and rough paths of this earth and yet to be enthroned with Christ at the Father's right hand, to laugh and cry with the children of this world and ceaselessly sing the praises of God with the choirs of angels—this is the life of the Christian until the morning of eternity breaks forth.

# III.2. Elevation of the Cross, September 14, 1939:
## *Ave Crux, Spes Unica!*
## [Hail Cross, Only Hope]

"Hail, Cross, our only hope!"—this is what the holy church summoned us to exclaim during the time for contemplating the bitter suffering of our Lord Jesus Christ. The jubilant exclamation of the Easter Alleluia silenced the serious song of the cross. But the sign of our salvation greeted us amid the time of Easter joy, since we were recalling the discovery of the One who had passed from sight. At the end of the cycle of ecclesiastical feasts, the cross greets us through the heart of the Savior. And now, as the church year draws toward an end, it is raised high before us and is to hold us spellbound until the Easter Alleluia summons us anew to forget the earth for a while and rejoice in the marriage of the Lamb.

Our holy Order has us begin our fast with the Exaltation of the Holy Cross. And it leads us to the foot of the cross to renew our holy vows. The Crucified One looks down on us and asks us whether we are still willing to honor what we promised in an hour of grace. And he certainly has reason to ask. More than ever the cross is a sign of contradiction. The followers of the Antichrist show it far more dishonor than did the Persians who stole it. They desecrate the images of the cross, and they make every effort to tear the cross out of the hearts of Christians. All too often they have succeeded even with those who, like us, once vowed to bear Christ's cross after him. Therefore, the Savior today looks at us, solemnly probing us, and asks each one of us: Will you remain faithful to the Crucified? Consider carefully! The world is in flames, the battle between Christ and the Antichrist has broken into the open. If you decide for Christ, it could cost you your life. Carefully consider what you promise. Taking and renewing vows is a dreadfully serious business. You make a promise to the Lord of heaven and earth. If you are not deadly serious about your will to fulfill it, you fall into the hands of the living God.

Before you hangs the Savior on the cross, because he became *obedient* unto death on the cross. He came into the world not to do his own will, but his Father's will. If you intend to be the bride of the Crucified, you too must completely renounce your own will and no longer have any desire except to fulfill God's will. He speaks to you in the holy Rule and the Constitutions of the Order. He speaks to you through the mouth of your superiors. He speaks to you by the gentle breath of the Holy Spirit in the depths of your heart. To remain true to your vow of obedience, you must listen to this voice day and night and follow its orders. However, this means daily and hourly crucifying your self-will and self-love.

The Savior hangs naked and destitute before you on the cross because he has chosen *poverty.* Those who want to follow him must renounce all earthly goods. It is not enough that you once left everything out there and came to the monastery. You must be serious about it now as well. Gratefully receive what God's providence sends you. Joyfully do without what he may let you to do without. Do not be concerned with your own body, with its trivial necessities and inclinations, but leave concern to those who are entrusted with it. Do not be concerned about the coming day and the coming meal.

The Savior hangs before you with a pierced heart. He has spilled his heart's blood to win your heart. If you want to follow him in holy *purity,* your heart must be free of every earthly desire. Jesus, the Crucified, is to be the only object of your longings, your wishes, your thoughts.

Are you now alarmed by the immensity of what the holy vows require of you? You need not be alarmed. What you have promised is indeed beyond your own weak, human power. But it is not beyond the power of the Almighty—this power will become yours if you entrust yourself to him, if he accepts your pledge of troth. He does so on the day of your holy profession and will do it anew today. It is the loving heart of your Savior that invites you to follow. It demands your obedience because the human will is blind and weak. It cannot find the way until it surrenders itself entirely to the divine will. He demands poverty because hands must be empty of earth's goods to receive the goods of heaven. He demands chastity because only the heart detached from all earthly love is free for the love of God. The arms of the Crucified are spread out to draw you to his heart. He wants your life in order to give you his.

*Ave Crux, Spes unica!*

The world is in flames. The conflagration can also reach our house. But high above all flames towers the cross. They cannot consume it. It is the path from earth to heaven. It will lift one who embraces it in faith, love, and hope into the bosom of the Trinity.

The world is in flames. Are you impelled to put them out? Look at the cross. From the open heart gushes the blood of the Savior. This extinguishes the flames of hell. Make your heart free by the faithful fulfillment of your vows; then the flood of divine love will be poured into your heart until it overflows and becomes fruitful to all the ends of the earth. Do you hear the groans of the wounded on the battlefields in the west and the east? You are not a physician and not a nurse and cannot bind up the wounds. You are enclosed in a cell and cannot get to them. Do you hear the anguish of the dying? You would like to be a priest and comfort them. Does the lament of the widows and orphans distress you? You would like to be an angel of mercy and help them. Look at the Crucified. If you are nuptially bound to him by the faithful observance of your holy vows, your *being* is precious blood. Bound to him, you are omnipresent as he is. You cannot help here or there like the physician, the nurse, the priest. You can be at all fronts, wherever there is grief, in the power of the cross. Your compassionate love takes you everywhere, this love from the divine heart. Its precious blood is poured everywhere—soothing, healing, saving.

The eyes of the Crucified look down on you—asking, probing. Will you make your covenant with the Crucified anew in all seriousness? What will you answer him? "Lord, where shall we go? You have the words of eternal life."

*Ave Crux, Spes unica!*

## III.3. The Marriage of the Lamb:
### For September 14, 1940

**V**enerunt nuptiae Agni et uxor eius praeparavit se (Rv 19:7). "The marriage of the Lamb has come and his Bride has prepared herself." This is certainly what echoed in our hearts on the eve of our holy profession and should be echoing again as we solemnly renew our holy vows. Mysterious words that conceal the deeply mysterious meaning of our holy vocation. Who is the Lamb? Who is the Bride? And what kind of marriage supper is this?

"And between the throne and the four living creatures and among the elders, I saw a Lamb standing, as though it had been slain" (Rv 5:6). When the seer of Patmos had this vision, the unforgettable day on the Jordan when John the Baptist showed him the "Lamb of God" who "takes away the sins of the world" (Jn 1:29) was still fresh in his memory. At that time, he had understood the word and now he understood the image. The One who had once walked along the Jordan and now appeared to him in white raiment with flaming eyes and a judge's sword, the "first and the last" (Rv 1:17)—he had in truth accomplished what the rites of the Old Covenant had suggested symbolically. When on the most momentous and holiest day of the year the high priest entered the Holy of Holies, into the supremely holy place of God's presence, he had previously taken two goats from the people: one on which to lay the people's sins, which were then carried out into the wilderness; the other to sprinkle its blood on the tent and ark of the covenant (Lv 16). This was the sin offering for the people. In addition, the priest had to provide a young bullock for himself and his house as a sin offering and a ram as a burnt offering. He also had to sprinkle the throne of grace with the blood of the bullock. When he had prayed, unseen by human eyes, for himself and his house and for all the people of Israel, he came out to the waiting people, and sprinkled the outer altar to cleanse it from his sins and those of the people. Then he sent the living goat into the wilderness, brought forward his own burnt offering and that of the people, and had the rest of the sin offering burned before the camp (and later before the gates). The Day of Atonement was a monumental and holy day. People remained in the holy place praying and fasting. And in the evening when everything had been accomplished, there was peace and joy in their hearts because God had taken away the burden of sin and given grace.

But what had effected the reconciliation? Not the blood of the slaughtered animals and not the high priest of Aaron's descent—St. Paul made this so compellingly clear in his letter to the Hebrews—but rather the real sacrifice of reconciliation that was anticipated in all these legally prescribed sacrifices, and the high priest after the order of Melchizedek, who was represented by the priests of Aaron's line. He was also the true Passover Lamb for whose sake the angel of death passed over the houses of the Hebrews when he slew the Egyptians. The Lord himself made the disciples understand this when he ate the lamb of sacrifice with them for the last time and then gave himself to them as food.

But why did he choose the lamb as the preferred symbol? Why did he continue to reveal himself in this form on the eternal throne of glory? Because he was innocent as a lamb and meek as a lamb; and because he came in order to allow himself to be led as a lamb to the slaughter (Is 53:7). This, too, John had witnessed when the Lord permitted himself to be bound at the Mount of Olives and nailed to the cross at Golgotha. There on Golgotha the true sacrifice of reconciliation was accomplished. Thereby the old sacrifices lost their efficacy; and soon they ceased entirely, as did also the old priesthood when the temple was destroyed. John had witnessed all of this, so he was not surprised at the Lamb on the throne. And because he was a faithful witness to the Lamb, the Bride of the Lamb was also shown to him.

He saw "the holy city, the new Jerusalem, descending out of heaven from God, prepared like a bride adorned for her husband" (Rv 21:2 and 9ff.). As Christ himself descended to earth from heaven, so too his Bride, the holy church, originated in heaven. She is born of the grace of God, indeed descended with the Son of God himself; she is inextricably bound to him. She is built of living stones; her cornerstone was laid when the Word of God assumed our human nature in the womb of the Virgin. At that time there was woven between the soul of the divine Child and the soul of the Virgin Mother the bond of the most intimate unity, which we call betrothal.

Hidden from the entire world, the heavenly Jerusalem had descended to earth. From this first joining in betrothal, there had to be born all the living building blocks to be used for the mighty structure: each individual soul awakened to life through grace. The Bridal Mother was to become the mother of all the redeemed. Like a spore from which new cells stream continually, she was to build up the living city of God. This hidden mystery was revealed to St. John as he stood beneath the cross with the Virgin Mother and was given over to her as her son. It was then that the church came into existence visibly; her hour had come, but not yet her perfection. She lives, she is wedded to the Lamb, but the hour of the solemn marriage supper will only arrive when the dragon has been completely conquered and the last of the redeemed have fought their battle to the end.

Just as the Lamb had to be killed to be raised upon the throne of glory, so the path to glory leads through suffering and the cross for everyone chosen to attend the marriage supper of the Lamb. All who want to be married to the Lamb must allow themselves to be fastened to the cross with him. Everyone marked by the blood of the Lamb is called to this, and that means all the baptized. But not everyone understands the call and follows it. There is a call to following more closely that resounds more urgently in the soul and demands a clear answer. This is the vocation to the religious life, and the answer is the religious vows.

For the person whom the Savior calls away from all natural ties— from one's family, one's people, and occupational circles—to cling to him alone, the bridal connection with the Savior also becomes more prominent than for the general host of the redeemed. They want to belong preeminently to the Lamb for all eternity, to follow him wherever he goes, and to sing the song of the virgins that no one else can sing (Rv 14:1-5).

When the attraction to religious life awakens in the soul, it is as if the Lord were courting her. And if she consecrates herself to him by profession of the vows and harkens to the *"Veni, sponsa Christi!"* ["Come, spouse of Christ!"], it is like an anticipation of the heavenly marriage feast. Nevertheless, this is but a prospect of the eternal feast of joy. The bridal happiness and fidelity of the soul consecrated to God must stand the test in open and hidden battles and in the everyday flow of religious life. The spouse whom she chooses is the Lamb that was slain. If she is to enter into heavenly glory with him, she must allow herself to be fastened to his cross. The three vows are the nails. The more willingly she stretches herself out on the cross and endures the blows of the hammer, the more deeply will she experience the reality of her union with the Crucified. Then being crucified itself becomes for her the marriage feast.

The vow of poverty opens one's hands so that they let go of everything they were clutching. It fastens them securely so they can no longer reach toward the things of this world. It should also bind the hands of the spirit and the soul: the desires, which again and again reach for pleasures and things; the cares that want to secure earthly life in every respect; busyness about many things, which endangers the one thing necessary. Living in superfluity and secure comfort contradicts the spirit of holy poverty and separates us from the poor Crucified One. Our sisters in the early times of the reform considered themselves happy when they lacked necessities. When the difficulties had been surmounted and enough of everything was at their disposal, they feared that the Lord had withdrawn from them. There is something wrong in a monastic community when concerns for the outer life take up so much time and energy that the spiritual life suffers. And there is something wrong in the soul of the individual religious who starts to take care of herself and to go after what she wants and likes instead of abandoning herself to divine providence and gratefully receiving what it gives her through the hands of the sisters in charge. Naturally, one should, after conscientious consideration, let the superior know what one's health requires. But having done that, one is relieved of further concern. The vow of holy poverty is intended to make us as carefree as the sparrows and the lilies so that our spirits and hearts may be free for God.

Holy obedience binds our feet so that they no longer go their own way, but God's way. Children of the world say they are free when they are not subject to another's will, when no one stops them from satisfying their wishes and inclinations. For this dream of freedom, they engage in bloody battles and sacrifice life and limb. The children of God see freedom as something else. They want to be unhindered in following the Spirit of God; and they know that the greatest hindrances do not come from without, but lie within us ourselves. Human reason and will, which would like so much to be their own masters, are unaware of their susceptibility to be swayed by natural inclinations and so to be enslaved by them. There is no better way of being freed of this slavery and receptive to the guidance of the Holy Spirit than that of holy obedience. In the poem of Goethe most informed by the Christian spirit, he has his heroine say, "Obedient, my soul felt free indeed." Genuine obedience is not content merely to avoid manifestly overstepping the prescriptions of Rule and Constitutions or the precepts of the superiors. It actually determines to deny one's own will. Therefore, the obedient person studies the Rule and the Constitutions, not to ferret out how many so-called "freedoms" are still permitted, but to recognize more and more how many small sacrifices are available daily and hourly as opportunities to advance in self-denial. Such a one takes them on as an easy yoke and a light burden, because doing so deepens the conviction of being closely bound to the Lord who was obedient to death on the cross. To the children of this world such action probably appears as useless, senseless, and petty. The Savior, who for thirty years filled his daily work with such small sacrifices, will judge differently.

The vow of chastity intends to release human beings from all the bonds of natural common life, to fasten them to the cross high above all the bustle, and to free their hearts for union with the Crucified. This sacrifice, too, is not accomplished once and for all. Of course, one is cut off, externally, from occasions that can become temptations outside, but often much that distracts the spirit and the heart, robbing them of their freedom, cleaves to the memory and fantasy. Besides, there is also a danger that new ties establish themselves within the protective cloister walls and hinder full union with the Divine Heart. When we enter the Order, we again become members of a family. We are to see and respect, as head and members of the Mystical Body of Christ, our superiors and the other sisters. But we are human, and something all too human can easily become mingled with holy, childlike, and sisterly love. We believe we see Christ in the people we look up to and fail to notice that we attach ourselves to them humanly and are in danger of losing sight of Christ. But human attraction is not the only cloud on purity of heart. Too little love is a worse offense against the Divine Heart than too much. Every aversion, any anger and resentment we tolerate in our hearts, closes the door to the Savior. Involuntary stirrings naturally arise through no fault of our own, but as soon as we become aware of them, we must relentlessly oppose them. Otherwise we resist God who is love and do the devil's work. The song sung by the virgins attending the Lamb is surely one of purest love.

The cross is again raised before us. It is the sign of contradiction. The Crucified looks down on us: "Are you also going to abandon me?" The day for the renewal of vows should always be one of serious self-examination. Have we lived up to the promises made in our first fervor? Have we lived in a manner befitting brides of the Crucified, the Lamb that was slain? In the last few months one has often heard the complaint that the many prayers for peace are still without effect. What right have we to be heard? Our desire for peace is undoubtedly genuine and sincere. But does it come from a completely purified heart? Have we truly prayed "in the name of Jesus," i.e., not just with the name of Jesus on our lips, but with the spirit and in the mind of Jesus, for the glory of the Father alone, without any self-seeking? The day on which God has unrestricted power over our hearts we shall also have unrestricted power over his. If we ponder this, we will no longer dare to judge anyone else. But neither will we be discouraged if, after living in the Order for a long time, we must admit we are still bunglers and beginners. The fountain from the heart of the Lamb has not dried up. We can wash our robes clean in it even today as the thief on Golgotha once did. Trusting in the atoning power of this holy fountain, we prostrate ourselves before the throne of the Lamb and answer his question: "Lord, to whom shall we go? You have the words of eternal life" (Jn 6:68). Let us draw from the springs of salvation for ourselves and for the entire parched world. Give us the grace to speak the bride's words with a pure heart: Come! Come, Lord Jesus. Come soon!

# III.4. Exaltation of the Cross
## September 14, 1941

In his *Holy Rule*, St. Benedict ordained that the fasts for religious begin with the feast of the Exaltation of the Cross. The long-extended Easter joy and the solemn feasts of summer—culminating in the crowning of the Queen of Heaven—could possibly cause the image of the Crucified to fade in us or to recede, as it remained hidden during the first centuries of Christianity. But when its time came, the cross appeared gleaming in the heavens, prompting the search for the buried and forgotten wood of humiliation that was to be recognized as the sign of salvation, the emblem of faith and the mark of the faithful. Every year, when the church again raises it before us, we are to recall the challenge of the Lord: Anyone who would follow me must take up his [or her] cross...! To take up one's cross means to go the way of penance and renunciation. For us religious, to follow the Savior means to allow ourselves to be fastened to the cross by the three nails of the holy vows. The Exaltation of the Cross and the renewal of vows belong together.

The Savior has preceded us on the way of poverty. All the goods in heaven and on earth belonged to him. They presented no danger to him; he could use them and yet keep his heart completely free of them. But he knew that it is scarcely possible for people to have possessions without succumbing to them and being enslaved by them. Therefore, he gave up everything and showed more by his example than by his counsel that only one who possesses nothing possesses everything. His birth in a stable, his flight to Egypt, already indicated that the Son of Man was to have no place to lay his head. Whoever follows him must know that we have no lasting dwelling here. The more deeply we feel this, the more zealous we are in striving for the future, and we rejoice at the thought that our citizenship is in heaven. Today it is good to reflect on the fact that poverty also includes the readiness to leave our beloved monastery itself. We have pledged ourselves to enclosure and do so anew when we renew our vows. But God did not pledge to leave us within the walls of the enclosure forever. He need not do so because he has other walls to protect us. This is similar to what he does in the sacraments. For us they are the prescribed means to grace, and we cannot receive them eagerly enough. But God is not bound to them. At the moment when some external force were to cut us off from receiving the sacraments, he could compensate us, superabundantly, in some other way; and he will do so all the more certainly and generously the more faithfully we have adhered to the sacraments previously. So it is also our holy duty to be as conscientious as possible in observing the precept of enclosure, to lead without hindrance a life hidden with Christ in God. If we are faithful and are then driven out into the street, the Lord will send his angels to encamp themselves around us, and their invisible pinions will enclose our souls more securely than the highest and strongest walls. We do not need to wish for this to happen. We may ask that the experience be spared us, but only with the solemn and honestly intended addition: Not mine, but your will be done! The vow of holy poverty is to be renewed without reservation.

Your will be done! This was the content of the Savior's life. He came into the world to fulfill the Father's will, not only to atone for the sin of disobedience through his obedience, but also to lead people back to their destiny by the way of obedience. The created will is not destined to be free to exalt itself. It is called to come into unison with the divine will. If it freely submits itself to this unison, then it is permitted in freedom to participate in the perfection of creation. If a free creature declines this unison, it lapses into bondage. The human will continues to retain the possibility of choice, but it is constrained by creatures that pull and pressure it in directions straying from the development of the nature desired by God, and so away from the goal toward which it itself was directed by its original freedom. With the loss of this original freedom, it also loses security in making decisions. It becomes unsteady and wavering, buffeted by doubt and scruples or obdurate in its error. There is no other remedy for this than the following of Christ, the Son of Man, who not only promptly obeyed his heavenly Father, but also subjected himself to people who imposed the Father's will on him. The obedience enjoined by God releases the enslaved will from the bonds of creatures and leads it back to freedom. Thus, it is also the way to purity of heart.

No chains of slavery are stronger than those of passion. Under its burden body, soul and spirit lose their strength and health, their clarity and beauty. Just as it is scarcely possible for one impaired by original sin to own things without clinging to them, so there is also the danger that any natural affection may degenerate into passion with all of its devastating consequences. God has provided two remedies for this: marriage and virginity. Virginity is the more radical and precisely therefore probably the easier way. But this is surely not the deepest reason Christ set us an example of it. Marriage is already a great mystery as the symbol of the bond between Christ and the church and at the same time as its instrument. But virginity is a still deeper mystery. It is not only the symbol and instrument of bridal union with Christ and of the union's supernatural fruitfulness, but also participates in the union. It originates in the depths of the divine life and leads back to it again. The eternal Father in unconditional love has given his entire being to his Son. And just as unconditionally does the Son give himself back to the Father. The passage of the God-Man through temporal life could alter nothing of this complete surrender of Person to Person. He belongs to the Father from eternity to eternity and could not give himself away to any human being. He could only incorporate the persons who wanted to give themselves to him into the unity of his Incarnate Divine Person as members of his Mystical Body and in this way bring them to the Father. This is why he came into the world. This is the divine fertility of his eternal virginity: that he can give souls supernatural life. And the fruitfulness of the virgins who follow the Lamb consists in the ability to assume the divine life in unmitigated strength and undivided surrender and, in union with the divine Head, pass it on to other souls, so awakening new members for the Head.

Divine virginity has a characteristic aversion to sin as the contrary of divine holiness. However, this aversion to sin gives rise to an indomitable love for sinners. Christ has come to tear sinners away from sin and to restore the divine image in defiled souls. He comes as the child of sin—his genealogy and the entire history of the Old Covenant show this—and he seeks the company of sinners so as to take all the sins of the world upon himself and carry them away to the infamous wood of the cross, which thereby precisely becomes the sign of his victory. This is precisely why virginal souls do not repulse sinners. The strength of their supernatural purity knows no fear of being sullied. The love of Christ impels them to descend into the darkest night. And no earthly maternal joy resembles the bliss of a soul permitted to enkindle the light of grace in the night of sins. The way to this is the cross. Beneath the cross the Virgin of virgins becomes the Mother of Grace.

Edith with her sister Rosa in the garden of the Echt Carmel, where
Rosa served for a time as portress of the community. Both were
arrested and deported to Auschwitz-Birkenau, where they died in
the gas chambers on August 9, 1942.

# IV

# *In the Grace of Vocation*

## IV.1. Three Addresses

### For the First Profession of
### Sister Miriam of Little St. Thérèse
### July 16, 1940

*Induit nos, Genetrix Domini, vestimento salutis: et indumento justitiae circumdedit nos, alleluia.* "The Mother of the Lord has clothed us in the robe of salvation: and she wraps about us the mantle of justice."

This is how we pray on the feast of the Queen of Carmel, on the solemn feast of our holy Order. For the Mother of God is the mediatrix of all grace. This is how every person, whom merciful love brings home after being lost, receives at her hand the garment of salvation, of sanctifying grace, and so is consecrated as a child of God. But on us who may call ourselves her children and sisters she confers another particular garment of salvation. As the Mother of the Lord, she chooses the souls she wishes to lead to her beloved Son and to bedeck with bridal robes for his honor and pleasure. She it is who planted her order on the lovely summit of Carmel as a garden of delight for the heavenly King, and then dispersed it throughout the entire world. As the sign of her special favor and her motherly protection, she has given us the holy scapular. She already gave it to Your Charity[1] a year ago along with the holy habit, but it was then only on loan to you for practice in arming yourself for God during the probationary period. Now you are receiving it anew, since you are allowed to enter into a sacred alliance with the Lord of heaven and earth. That this holy celebration is combined with the feast of the Queen of Heaven is evidence of special maternal love, just as it was a special sign of love that the Mother of God gave you her own name.

Such special proofs of being loved oblige one to show special gratitude. When we receive the holy habit of Carmel, we pledge ourselves not only to extraordinary service to our divine Bridegroom, but also to his holy Mother. The *garment of salvation* is also called the *mantle of justice*. We are clothed in it with the instruction that we are to put off the old person and put on the new, who is created in the image of God in holiness and righteousness. By *righteousness* the Scriptures mean perfection, the condition of the justified person who is made *right* again as she or he was before the Fall. By taking on the garment of righteousness, we thus oblige ourselves to strive for perfection with all our strength and to preserve the holy garment intact. There is no better way to serve the Queen of Carmel and to show her our gratitude than by contemplating her example and following her on the way of perfection.

Only a few words from the Virgin Mary have come down to us in the Gospels. But these few words are like heavy grains of pure gold. When they melt in the ardor of loving meditation, they more than suffice to bathe our entire lives in a luminous golden glow.

The first word that we hear in the conversation with the angel at the Annunciation to Mary is, "How shall this happen, since I know not man?" It is the simple recognition of her *virginal purity*. She had consecrated her whole heart and all the strength of her body, soul, and spirit to the service of God in undivided surrender. Thereby she pleased the Almighty. He accepted her surrender and blessed her with wonderful fruitfulness by raising her to be the Mother of God. She looked deeply into the mystery of virginity of which her divine Son later said, "Whoever can accept this, ought to do so." Her heart exulted in glory as she discovered what God had prepared for those who love him. She can give her beloved ones nothing better than a call to follow this way on which they, too, will attain wonderful fruitfulness and a blessedness beyond all imagining. As the symbol of the radiant beauty encompassing a truly virginal soul, she wraps the white mantle around you. It is to remind us always that we are invited to the marriage of the Lamb, called to sing in the choir of virgins that holy hymn of heavenly love that no one else can sing, and to follow the Lamb constantly without ever being separated from him.

As soon as the angel had heard Mary's avowal, he immediately dispelled her hesitation. God was not thinking of dispensing her from her vow. No, it is precisely because of her virginity that she is receptive to the overshadowing of the Holy Spirit that makes her fruitful. She is to become the virgin mother. And now we hear the Virgin's second word, "Behold, I am the handmaid of the Lord. Be it done to me according to your word." This is the most perfect expression of *obedience*. Being obedient means to listen to the word of someone else in order to submit one's own will to that of another. It is a virtue and in fact a discipline of justice when the other is a superior who is better able than we are ourselves to guide us to what is right.

Here justice [or righteousness] does not mean full perfection, but rather the cardinal virtue that gives to each his own. Truly perfect obedience is the obedience given to the Almighty, the subordination of one's own will to that of God. Jesus has given us the example of this perfect obedience, for he came not to do his own will but the will of him who sent him. And the Virgin practiced this perfect obedience when she called herself a handmaid of the Lord and actually was such, prepared to put all her faculties at the service of the Lord.

To this obedience we, too, oblige ourselves by our holy vow of obedience. We oblige ourselves to subject our own will to that of our superiors in the belief that the Lord himself speaks to us through their mouths and reveals his will to us. And who could know our needs better than he? So the way of obedience is the surest way to our eternal goal. And though full perfection does not lie in it alone, obedience remains the key to it. God, after all, wants our salvation, and when our will is in full unison with his, we can be certain that we will reach perfection. Jesus and Mary are also examples of this subjection of the will to an authority and order given by God: In silent obedience, both of them follow, at the slightest indication, him whom the heavenly Father has given to the Holy Family as a visible superior. They faithfully fulfilled the commands of the law that the Lord had established for his people and observed the regulations of spiritual and civil authorities.

As a sign of such a binding of the will, we receive this cincture, while we are addressed by the words that Christ spoke to St. Peter, "When you were younger, you girded yourself and went where you pleased. When you are older, another will gird you." Whoever allows herself to be led like a child in the harness of holy obedience will reach the kingdom of God that is promised to the little ones.

Obedience led the royal daughter of the house of David to the simple little house of the poor carpenter of Nazareth. Obedience led both of these most holy people away from the secure enclosure of this modest home onto the highway and into the stable at Bethlehem. It laid the Son of God in the manger. In freely chosen *poverty* the Savior and his mother wandered the streets of Judea and Galilee and lived on the alms of the faithful. Naked and exposed, the Lord hung on the cross and left the care of his mother to the love of his disciple. Therefore, he demands poverty of those who would follow him. The heart must be free of ties to earthly goods, of concern about them, dependence on them, desire for them, if it is to belong to the divine Bridegroom exclusively, if the will intends to follow every suggestion of holy obedience in unreserved readiness.

The three sacred vows supplement one another and require one another. One cannot fulfill any one of them completely without at the same time observing the others. The Mother of God has gone before us on this way and will be our guide on this way. Entrust yourself in childlike surrender to this loving Mother, dear Sister Miriam. Then Your Charity need not be frightened before the exalted immensity of what you have promised. The Lord who has called you and today accepts you as his bride will give you the grace to persevere in your calling and will give it through the hands of his Mother. And there is still another patroness at your side. St. Thérèse of the Child Jesus shows you even in the little details of daily life how one can follow him and Mary in Carmel. If you learn from her to depend on God alone and serve him with a wholly pure and detached heart, then you can join with your whole soul in singing the jubilant song of the holy Virgin, "My soul proclaims the greatness of the Lord, and my spirit rejoices in God my Savior. For he has done great things for me, and holy is his name." And like little St. Thérèse you will be able to say at the end, "I do not regret that I have given myself to love."

## The Hidden Life and Epiphany

When the gentle light of the advent candles begins to shine in the dark days of December—a mysterious light in a mysterious darkness—it awakens in us the consoling thought that the divine light, the Holy Spirit, has never ceased to illumine the darkness of the fallen world. He has remained faithful to his creation, regardless of all the infidelity of creatures. And if the darkness would not allow itself to be penetrated by the heavenly light, there were nevertheless some places always predisposed for it to blaze.

A ray from this light fell into the hearts of our original parents even during the judgment to which they were subjected. This was an illuminating ray that awakened in them the knowledge of their guilt, an enkindling ray that made them burn with fiery remorse, purifying and cleansing, and made them sensitive to the gentle light of the star of hope, which shone for them in the words of promise of the "proto-evangelium," the original gospel.

As were the hearts of the first human beings, so down through the ages again and again human hearts have been struck by the divine ray. Hidden from the whole world, it illuminated and irradiated them, let the hard, encrusted, misshapen matter of these hearts soften, and then with the tender hand of an artist formed them anew into the image of God. Seen by no human eye, this is how living building blocks were and are formed and brought together into a church first of all invisible. However, the visible church grows out of this invisible one in ever new, divine deeds and revelations that shed their light—ever new *epiphanies*. The silent working of the Holy Spirit in the depths of the soul made the patriarchs into friends of God. However, when they came to the point of allowing themselves to be used as his pliant instruments, he established them in an external visible efficacy as bearers of historical development, and awakened from among them his chosen people. Therefore Moses, too, was educated quietly and then sent as the leader and lawgiver.

Not everyone whom God uses as an instrument must be prepared in this way. People may also be instruments of God without their knowledge and even against their will, possibly even people who neither externally nor interiorly belong to the church. They would then be used like the hammer or chisel of the artist, or like a knife with which the vine-dresser prunes the vines. For those who belong to the church, outer membership can also temporally precede interior, in fact can be materially significant for it (as when someone without faith is baptized and then comes to faith through the public life in the church). But it finally comes down to the interior life; formation moves from the inner to the outer. The deeper a soul is bound to God, the more completely surrendered to grace, the stronger will be its influence on the form of the church. Conversely, the more an era is engulfed in the night of sin and estrangement from God the more it needs souls united to God. And God does not permit a deficiency. The greatest figures of prophecy and sanctity step forth out of the darkest night. But for the most part the formative stream of the mystical life remains invisible. Certainly the decisive turning points in world history are substantially co-determined by souls whom no history book ever mentions. And we will only find out about those souls to whom we owe the decisive turning points in our personal lives on the day when all that is hidden is revealed.

Because hidden souls do not live in isolation, but are a part of the living nexus and have a position in a great divine order, we speak of an invisible church. Their impact and affinity can remain hidden from themselves and others for their entire earthly lives. But it is also possible for some of this to become visible in the external world. This is how it was with the persons and events intertwined in the mystery of the Incarnation. Mary and Joseph, Zechariah and Elizabeth, the shepherds and the kings, Simeon and Anna—all of these had behind them a solitary life with God and were prepared for their special tasks before they found themselves together in those awesome encounters and events and, in retrospect, could understand how the paths left behind led to this climax. Their astounded adoration in the presence of these great deeds of God is expressed in the songs of praise that have come down to us.

In the people who are gathered around the manger, we have an analogy for the church and its development. Representatives of the old royal dynasties to whom the savior of the world was promised and representatives of faithful people constitute the relationship between the Old and the New Covenants. The kings from the faraway East indicate the Gentiles for whom salvation is to come from Judea. So here there is already "the church made up of Jews and Gentiles." The kings at the manger represent seekers from all lands and peoples. Grace led them before they ever belonged to the external church. There lived in them a pure longing for truth that did not stop at the boundaries of native doctrines and traditions. Because God is truth and because he wants to be found by those who seek him with their whole hearts, sooner or later the star had to appear to show these *wise men* the way to truth. And so they now stand before the Incarnate Truth, bow down and worship it, and place their crowns at its feet, because all the treasures of the world are but a little dust compared to it.

And the kings have a special meaning for us, too. Even though we already belonged to the external church, an interior impulse nevertheless drove us out of the circle of inherited viewpoints and conventions. We knew God, but we felt that he desired to be sought and found by us in a new way. Therefore we wanted to open ourselves and sought for a star to show us the right way. And it arose for us in the grace of vocation. We followed it and found the divine infant. He stretched out his hands for our gifts. He wanted the pure *gold* of a heart detached from all earthly goods; the *myrrh* of a renunciation of all the happiness of this world in exchange for participation in the life and suffering of Jesus; the *frankincense* of a will that surrenders itself and strains upward to lose itself in the divine will. In return for these gifts, the divine child gave us himself.

But this admirable exchange was not a one-time event. It fills our entire lives. After the solemn hour of bridal surrender, there followed the everyday life of observance in the Order. We had to "return to our own country," but "taking another way" and escorted by the new light that had blazed up for us at those solemn places. The new light commands us to search anew. "God lets himself be sought," says St. Augustine, "to let himself be found. He lets himself be found to be sought again." After each great hour of grace, it is as if we were but beginning now to understand our vocation. Therefore an interior need prompts us to renew our vows repeatedly. That we do so on the feast of the three kings whose pilgrimage and affirmation are for us a symbol for our lives has a deep meaning. To each authentic, heartfelt renewal of vows, the divine Child responds with renewed acceptance and a deeper union. And this means a new, hidden operation of grace in our souls. Perhaps it is revealed in an epiphany, the work of God becoming visible in our external behavior and activity noticed by those around us. But perhaps it also bears fruit that, though observed, conceals from all eyes the mysterious source from which its vital juices pour.

Today we live again in a time that urgently needs to be renewed at the hidden springs of God-fearing souls. Many people, too, place their last hope in these hidden springs of salvation. This is a serious warning cry: Surrender without reservation to the Lord who has called us. This is required of us so that the face of the earth may be renewed. In faithful trust, we must abandon our souls to the sovereignty of the Holy Spirit. It is not necessary that we experience the epiphany in our lives. We may live in confident certainty that what the Spirit of God secretly effects in us bears its fruits in the kingdom of God. We will see them in eternity.

So this is how we want to bring our gifts to the Lord: We lay them in the hands of the Mother of God. This first Saturday[1] is particularly dedicated to her honor, and nothing can give her most pure heart greater joy than an ever deeper surrender to the Divine Heart. Furthermore, she will certainly have no more urgent petition for the Child in the manger than the one for holy priests and a richly blessed priestly ministry. And this is the petition today's Saturday for priests bids us make and our Holy Mother has enjoined on us so compellingly as an essential constituent of our vocation to Carmel.

## For January 6, 1941

Again we kneel with the three kings at the manger. The heartbeat of the Divine Child has guided the star that led us here. Its light, the reflection of the eternal light, is variously distributed in the rays around the heads of the saints whom the church shows us as the court of the new-born King of Kings. They allow something of the mystery of our vocation to flash before us.

Mary and Joseph are not to be separated from their Divine Child in the Christmas liturgy. During this time, they do not have a feast of their own, because all the feasts of the Lord are *their* feasts, feasts of the Holy Family. They do not *come* to the manger, but are there to begin with. Whoever comes to the Child also comes to them. They are completely imbued with his heavenly light.

Closest to the newborn Savior we see St. Stephen. What secured the first martyr of the Crucified this place of honor? In youthful enthusiasm he accomplished what the Lord said upon his entrance into the world, "A body you have prepared for me. Behold, I come to fulfill your will." He practiced complete *obedience* that is rooted in love and revealed in love. He followed the Lord in what may be by nature the most difficult for the human heart, and even seems impossible: He fulfilled the command to love one's enemies as did the Savior himself. The Child in the manger, who has come to fulfill his Father's will even to death on the cross, sees before him in spirit all who will follow him on this way. His heartbeat goes out to the youth whom he will one day await with a palm as the first to reach the Father's throne. His little hand points him out to us as an example, as if to say, "See the *gold* that I expect of you."

Not far from the first martyr stand the *flores martyrum*, the tender buds that were broken before they had ripened to the act of sacrifice. There is a pious belief that the grace of natural maturity came to the innocent children beforehand and gave them an understanding of what was happening to them so they could give themselves freely and thus be ensured martyrdom. Even so, they do not resemble the valiant confessor who heroically took on the cause of Christ. In their defenseless surrender, they are much more like lambs led to the slaughter. So they are the example of uttermost *poverty*. They have no other goods than their lives. And now even that is taken from them, and they allow it to happen without resistance. They surround the manger to show us what kind of *myrrh* we are to bring to the Divine Child: Those who want to belong entirely to him must deliver themselves to him in complete self-renunciation, surrender to the divine decision like these children.

Neither will the Savior allow him who was particularly dear to him during his life, the disciple whom Jesus loved, to be absent from the manger. He is entrusted to us as the example of *virginal purity*. Because he was pure, he pleased the Lord. He was allowed to rest on the heart of Jesus to be initiated there into the secrets of the Divine Heart. As the heavenly Father witnessed to his Son when he cried out, "This is My beloved Son, listen to him!", so the Divine Child also seems to point to the beloved disciple and to say, "No *frankincense* is more pleasing to me than the loving submission of a pure heart. Listen to him who was permitted to look at God because he was pure of heart." No one has looked more deeply into the hidden abyss of the divine life than he. Therefore, he proclaims the mystery of the eternal birth of the Divine Word in the liturgy each feast day during the days of Christmas and continues to do so at the end of daily Mass.[1] He participated in the struggles of his Lord as only a soul with bridal love could. He has drawn for us the Good Shepherd who goes after lost sheep. We can learn from John how precious human souls are to the Divine Heart and how we can give him no greater joy than by being willing instruments on his shepherding way. He has carefully preserved and transmitted to us passages in which the Savior witnessed to himself and made known his divinity before friends and foes. He has disclosed to us the shrine of the Divine Heart by recording for us the Lord's farewell address and his high priestly prayer. Through John we know how we are to participate as our destiny in the life of Christ—as a branch of the divine vine—and in the life of the triune God. While he was still alive, he was permitted to see the Incarnate God as the judge of the world in order to paint for us the mighty, enigmatic images of the mysterious revelation of the final days. He showed us this in that book which, like none other, can teach us to understand the chaos of this time as a part of the great battle between Christ and the Antichrist, a book of relentless solemnity and consoling promise.

John at the manger of the Lord—this says to us: See what happens to those who give themselves to God with pure hearts. In return, as a royal gift, they may participate in the entire inexhaustible fullness of Jesus' incarnate life. Come and drink from the springs of living water that the Savior releases to the thirsty and that stream to eternal life. The Word has become flesh and lies before us in the form of a little newborn child. We may come to him and bring him the gifts of our holy vows. And then, in a new year, we should go with him the entire way of his life on earth. Every mystery of this life that we seek to discern in loving contemplation is for us a fount of eternal life. And the same Savior, whom the written word presents to our eyes on all the paths he trod on earth in human form, lives among us disguised in the form of the eucharistic bread. He comes to us every day as the bread of life. In either of these forms he is near to us; in either of these forms he wants to be sought and found by us. The one supports the other. When we see that Savior before us with the eyes of faith as the Scriptures portray him, then our desire to receive him in the bread of life increases. The eucharistic bread, on the other hand, awakens our desire to get to know the Lord in the written word more and more deeply and strengthens our spirit to get a better understanding.

A new year at the hand of the Lord—we do not know whether we shall experience the end of this year. But if we drink from the fount of the Savior each day, then each day will lead us deeper into eternal life and prepare us to throw off the burdens of this life easily and cheerfully at some time when the call of the Lord sounds. The Divine Child offers us his hand to renew our bridal bond. Let us hurry to clasp this hand. The Lord is my light and my salvation—of whom shall I be afraid?

# IV.2. Three Dialogues

## *I Am Always in Your Midst*

**M**other Ursula (Superior, kneeling before an altar with a picture or statue of St. Angela Merici[1]):
As I've done so often, I come to you at night,
Oh faithful mother, to pour into your good heart
The heavy burden of cares.
In the noise of day I am less aware of them.
Then tasks press upon me, people come,
They call me here; they call me there.
Everyone wants advice and comfort and help from this one—
The neediest of all, who from herself
Can do nothing at all, and only from God's hand
Receives from moment to moment
What at that time she needs for them.
There is no time or space left for concerns about the future.
Then at night the still cell surrounds me
That is greatly loved and so often longed for earnestly.
Then out of the darkness there creeps something like a dark shadow
That whispers anxious questions to my ears:
The great host of daughters, richly gifted,
By long efforts appropriately equipped
To work gladly in the service of the Lord;
Full of burning desire to ignite
God's light in young human souls,
As their holy vocation requires—
What is to become of them if suddenly
All of this should end, and when our vineyard
Passes from our hands to others?
What will become of them, become of our young people?
What am I to do, tell me, when young souls come
Knocking for entrance eagerly and in high spirits
Because God's call points them to his way?
May I consecrate their lives to an uncertain fate?

116

Saint Angela (speaks from the picture):
>    You could indeed give the answer yourself,
>    Have often enough, when others questioned you like this,
>    Led them to clarity and peace.
>    But I know well that one is wise for others
>    And for oneself as helpless as a child.
>    That's why it's right for you to come to mother,
>    And I will gladly help you bear your burden
>    You who bear the burdens of so many.

Mother Ursula:
>    How good it feels to become a child again
>    And rest without cares in mother's arms.
>    The gentle hand drives off the fever's heat,
>    And every pain is lessened before the tender eyes.
>    Will you now advise me what to do?
>    I'll listen calmly and obey, oh so gladly!

Saint Angela:
>    Let's do it as in your schools:
>    There the teacher is quiet and the student speaks.
>    What do you think has made your mother great
>    And pleasing in the eyes of God?
>    What has evoked blessing on her work?

Mother Ursula:
>    What an immense question for a little child!
>    Are not God's thoughts about us actually
>    As high above us as the dome of heaven?
>    But I will risk the answer that occurs to me.
>    From tenderest youth, you have listened
>    To every stirring in the depths of your soul
>    That is only perceived in deepest silence.
>    And like a creature that without turning
>    Goes sometimes forward, sometimes back, freely winged,
>    Even, according to the Spirit's movement that drives it,
>    So you follow the call of the tender voice,
>    A willing instrument in the Lord's hand.

Saint Angela:
>    I listened to his word—of course,
>    That's true. And it is also true
>    That I would gladly be his instrument.
>    But don't you know that the day was already waning,

That I didn't see the way clearly until evening?
Did I not lose much time by hesitating?

Mother Ursula:
You put me to the test, but it seems to me
As though now I've found the proper guiding thread.
In unswerving faithfulness you waited
Patiently year by year; not right nor left
Did you swerve from the path, though in the dark night
It always remained hidden from your sight.
Like that star that once led the wise men,
Above your head there shone the lofty goal
That early on had already won your young heart,
And then radiated in ever new clarity.
Hidden from the world, you persisted
Like our dear Lord, who for thirty years
In a narrow orbit spent his time
Doing lowly work according to human standards,
Instead of mighty deeds to earn great fame.
Even longer than he himself you remained in silence,
And in the silence God's work ripened.

Saint Angela:
You've recognized it: that is what God likes—
Patient waiting till the hour comes
That he determines; in the dark to wander
As the Spirit's quiet movement leads us,
And unseen by human eyes,
To gather the flowers that bloom along the path.
The little buds daily given us at the hand of the Mother
Of the Son of God—
He takes them to his heart: there they bloom
And never wither; their fragrance
Spreads sweet and strong with wonderful healing power,
Over all the world, closing wounds
That people's "mighty deeds" produce in it.

Mother Ursula:
This is the "little way" of great wisdom
That the flower of Carmel taught us.
Now I see that it is our way, too,
As it was yours for the longest time.
External action in a definite form,
To which we are accustomed, that we trust and love,

It is not reality, it can shatter—
And maybe it is then that first the essence is revealed.
We will remain faithful at our posts
As long as it is pleasing to our Lord and God.
And our efforts will be as diligent
As if we never had to think about an end.
But if tomorrow or the next day
He takes our cherished work from our busy hands,
We will recognize that he can get along without us, too;
And willingly we follow where he leads—
Be it to Egypt, be it to Nazareth.

Saint Angela:
Now where is the concern for your daughters?
Are you as sure that they too understand
The way that now is in your sight?
The young energies that want to get moving,
How are you going to steer them onto a new road?

Mother Ursula:
You do not frighten me with this probing question.
To be sure, I cannot say in a single word
How I would help myself if I could;
But I think that if I carry in my heart
With very special love each soul
That God entrusts to me, as you command
And strongly suggest to every mother,
Then at the right moment the Spirit will
Show me what is needed for each one.
Of course, the Lord leads each on her own path,
And what we call "fate" is the artist's doing,
The eternal Artist, who creates material for himself
And forms it into images in various ways:
By gentle finger strokes and also by chisel blows.
But he does not work on dead material;
His greatest creative joy in fact is
That under his hand the image stirs,
That life pours forth to meet him.
The life that he himself has placed in it
And that now answers him from within
To chisel blows or quiet finger stroke.
So we collaborate with God on his work of art.
But not just ourselves does he allow us thus to form

According to his suggestion: often a person does not hear
The soft voice that speaks within.
Perhaps she hears the soft beating of the wings
Of the dove, but does not understand where its flight
Is drawing her. Then someone else must come,
Gifted with a finer ear attuned and keener sight,
And disclose the meaning of the obscure words.
This is the guide's wonderful gift,
The highest that, according to a sage's word,
The Creator has given to the creation:
To be his fellow worker in the salvation of souls.

Saint Angela:

Then build God's kingdom
According to the wonderful fluttering of his Spirit,
And be sure that nothing will be lacking.
The vineyard that demands your efforts,
Even if it be a different one than up to now,
A different one than you yourself had thought.
Then you have one more question to resolve
To which you sought an answer tonight:
May you bind still other human beings
To an uncertain fate?

Mother Ursula:

How foolish now this doubt appears to me!
If God's call sounds within a soul,
When he leads it to our house's door
And to knock hard—why should we not open
The door wide, our arms and our heart?
If he shows the way, then he also knows
That it is not a wrong track where people suddenly get lost;
No spurious way that ends in desert sands.
That step by step the road will be revealed,
I firmly believe. And in fact what is certain?
Where is "certain fate"? Yes, we see—
And it's good that we are so confronted—
How around us structures are becoming ruins
That seemed to us to have been raised for eternity.
One thing alone is certain: that God is
And that his hand holds us in being.
Then even if around us the whole world falls to wrack and ruin,
We are not ruined if we hold ourselves to him.

Saint Angela:
> Hold fast to this and so fortify those who are yours.
> Morning is dawning, a new day is breaking.

Mother Ursula:
> I greet it as though reborn
> With its young light. I thank you
> For your attentive solace during this night.
> Oh, how faithfully you fulfill the promise
> That you once made at your departure
> To remain forever in our midst
> With Christ, our heavenly spouse!
> Therefore even now I won't say goodbye to you.
> The voice may be silent that came to me
> Tonight with a motherly tone.
> Yet I know the mother is always at my side.
> With her blessing, I go into the day.

## Te Deum Laudamus [We Praise Thee]:
## For December 7, 1940 [Feast of St. Ambrose]

Ambrose (kneeling in his room before the opened Holy Scriptures):
    Now the last one is gone. I thank you, O Lord,
    For this quiet hour in the night.
    You know how much I like to serve your flock;
    I want to be a good shepherd to your lambs,
    That's why this door is open day and night,
    And anyone can enter unannounced.
    Oh, how much suffering and bitter need is brought in here—
    The burden becomes almost too great for this father's heart.
    But you, my God, you surely know our weakness
    And at the right time remove the yoke from our shoulders.
    You give me rest, and from this book,
    The holy book, you speak to me
    And pour new strength into my soul.
        (He opens it, makes a great sign of the cross,
            and begins to read silently.)

Augustine (appears in the door and remains standing, hesitant):
    He is alone—I could go to him
    And let him know the struggles of my heart.
    But he is speaking with his God,
    Seeking rest and refreshment in the Scriptures
    After a long day's work and care.
    Oh no, I'll not disturb him.
    I'll kneel down a little here;
    Then I'll surely take something of his peace with me.
        (He kneels.)

Ambrose (looks up):
    What was that? Didn't I hear a rustling at the door?
        (He gets up.)
    Come closer, friend, you who come at night.
    In the dark I cannot see who you are.
        (He goes to the door with the lamp.)

122

Is it possible? Augustine? Peace be with you!
You dear, infrequent guest, please do come in.
(He takes him by the hand, leads him in, shows him a seat,
and sits down facing him.)

Augustine:

Oh, how your goodness shames me, holy man!
I really have not earned such a welcome.

Ambrose:

Don't you remember how happily I greeted you
When you stood here before me for the first time?
You, the star of oratory
That stirred Carthage to amazement,
That did not even find its match in Rome,
I was happy to see
Within the confines of my Milan.

Augustine:

Oh, if you had only seen into my heart!
I wasn't worthy to be seen by you.

Ambrose:

I saw you often when I spoke to the people.
Your burning eye hung on my lips.

Augustine:

Your mouth overflowed with heavenly wisdom.
But I was not interested in wisdom.
I did not come for wisdom.
I only heard how you put together the *words;*
Only an orator's magic power attracted me.
That, *what* you spoke—Christ's holy doctrine—
I wasn't eager to know, it seemed like vanity to me,
Already refuted by my teachers long ago.
But while I listened to the *words* alone,
I was drawn—I hardly noticed it—into the *meaning.*
*One* word of Scripture oft repeated
Deeply affected me and gave me much to think about:
"The letter deadens," you said, "the spirit gives life."
When the Manichæans laughed over the Word of Christ,
Was not this because those fools
Only understood what they were reading literally,
While the spirit remained sealed to them?

Ambrose:

>But the Holy Spirit's ray fell on you.
>Thank him who freed you from error's chains,
>And thank her, too, who interceded for you.
>O Augustine, thank God for your mother.
>She is your angel before the eternal throne;
>Her commerce is in heaven, and her petitions
>Fall, like steady drops, heavily into the bowl
>Of compassion.

Augustine:

>Yes, I surely know—what would I have become without her?
>Oh, how many hot tears did I cost her,
>I, her unfaithful son, who really don't deserve it!

Ambrose:

>Therefore, she now weeps sweet tears of joy,
>And she is richly rewarded for all her suffering.

Augustine:

>She already wept tears of joy when she perceived
>That I had escaped the Manichæan net.
>I was still deep in night, tormented by doubts.
>But she assured me optimistically
>That the day of peace was now no longer far away.
>While still alive, she was to see me entirely safe.

Ambrose:

>The Lord himself probably gave her certainty.
>Her firm faith did not mislead her.

Augustine:

>But I still had a long way to go.
>My teaching post had become unbearable for me.
>The frivolous game of the orator's art rankled me.
>I sought truth, and I no longer desired to waste
>The spirit of my youth in colorful pretense.
>From Milan I fled into isolation.
>My spirit brooded in unrest.

Ambrose:

>I waited here for you—how much I wanted
>With God's help to guide you to the harbor!

Augustine:

> Oh, how often I stood here on this threshold!
> You did not see. There came crowds of people
> Who sought help from the good shepherd.
> I looked on for a little while and then silently went away.
> At times I also came upon you alone, like today,
> Immersed in the study of your beloved books.
> Then I did not risk shortening your meager rest.
> I knelt here a little near you
> And discreetly slipped away. Today, too,
> It would have happened thus if you had not discovered me.

Ambrose:

> Thank my angel who led my eye to you.
> But tell me now what brought you here.

Augustine:

> I already wrote you that God's ray lit on me.
> Before my eyes stood all the misery of my life.
> It choked me, clamped my chest,
> I could no longer breathe at home
> And fled out into the open.
> In the garden I sought a quiet place,
> Fled into the presence of the faithful friend himself.
> Finally, a stream of tears burst forth.
> Then from a neighbor's house there urged itself on me
> A child's voice singing clearly.
> I heard the words, "Take and read."
> Again and again it rang in my ears
> As children endlessly repeat.
> But to me it comes from another world:
> It is the call of the Lord! I leap up
> And rush to Alypius who is still sitting and thinking.
> The book lies beside him where I was reading it.
> I open it. There stands for me the instruction;
> I found it clear in the Apostle's word:
> "Give up feasting and carousing at last,
> Arise from the bed of soft sensory lust.
> Renounce all the contention of frivolous ambition.
> Look instead at Jesus Christ, the Lord."
> Then the night receded, and day began—
> I took to the road in the presence of the Lord,
> My friend Alypius hand in hand with me.

Ambrose:

>Thank God, who had mercy on you!
>How wonderful are your ways, Lord!

Augustine:

>I wrote to you and asked for your advice.
>You recommended to me a good teacher.
>In the prophecy of Isaiah I found
>The servant of God, the lamb, that suffered for us.
>And things grew brighter and brighter in my eyes.
>We did not rush, yet let us now speak to you
>In longing and in humility:
>Lead us to the baptismal font and wash us clean.

Ambrose:

>Oh, bless you, my beloved son!
>There is no one whom I have led with greater joy
>To the holy bath that gives new life.
>Come soon and bring me your faithful friend.

Augustine:

>There is yet a third person whom we are leading to you:
>Adeodatus, my beloved child.
>No doubt a child of sin through my fault;
>But now the child of grace through God's goodness.
>He is a youth, almost still a boy in years,
>But with more wisdom than his father.
>He brings the Lord an undefiled heart,
>And it is pure hearts who see God.

Ambrose:

>So soon a thrice-blessed day will beam for us.
>O Augustine, don't look back into the dark anymore.
>Before me now radiant lies your path.
>The light that God ignited in your heart,
>Will shine brightly into the farthest times,
>The whole church will be filled with it.
>And countless hearts will be inflamed
>By the love consuming your great heart.
>Oh look with me up to the throne
>Of the thrice Holy One!
>Don't you hear the choir of holy spirits?
>They sing their holy songs of praise

Full of thanks in inexpressibly great joy,
Because the lost son has found his way to the Father.
    (Both stand listening; then Ambrose intones:)

Ambrose:
    *Te Deum...*

Augustine (sings the second half-verse, then alternately together
    with the invisible choirs.)

## Conversation at Night

**Mother** (at night in her cell, having fallen asleep while writing; awakens with a start):
The pen fell from my tired hand.
So much I still intended to do today.
Yet midnight is near and nature
Demands her due and won't be pressured.
I'll try to finish just this *one* letter.
  (Writes a little; her head again sinks onto the table—
  two clangs of the bell—she jumps up):
The turn[1] now in the middle of the night?
  (Someone knocks.)
Now there's a rapping at the door—it's opening. My Jesus, help!

**A feminine form** (enters, dressed like a pilgrim; speaks):
Peace be with you!
Oh, don't be afraid! What's approaching you at night
Is a supplicant who has no other weapons
Than raised hands.

**Mother:**
Oh, so speak!
I'll gladly do whatever you ask
If it's within my power. The fear has vanished.
Your word is mild and your expression peaceful.
It seems to me to be coming from eternity,
And it arouses a longing for heaven in my heart.
So come and rest. You've surely traveled a long way.
  (Points her to a seat.)

**Stranger:**
Thank you for your goodness. Yes, I have traveled far
From land to land and from door to door.
I am seeking lodgings.

128

Mother:

Looking for lodgings? How the word touches me!
I am reminded of that pure one, the Immaculate,
Who once about this time also sought lodgings.
(Kneels down):
Oh tell me! Are you she herself, the Virgin Mother?

Stranger (raises her up):

I am not she—but I know her very well,
And it is my joy to serve her.
I am of her people, her blood,
And once I risked my life for this people.
You recall her when you hear my name.
My life serves as a image of hers for you.

Mother:

A riddle, unusually hard to understand—
How am I to grasp it?
You are a woman whom we recognize as an "example"?
You staked your life for your people?
And you certainly had no weapon, either, then,
Except those hands raised in supplication?
So are you Esther, then, the queen?

Esther:

That is what people called me. You know my fate.

Mother:

As much as is in the holy books.
It always touched me: As a tender child
You lost your father and your mother.

Esther:

The good uncle was father to me and mother.
But no—he led me to the real Father,
The Father of all of us high in heaven.
My uncle's heart burned hot with passion,
In holy ardor for God and for his people.
He raised me for them. So I grew up
Far from home and yet protected
As in the temple's quiet sanctuary.
I read the holy Scriptures of these people,
Who were now enslaved in a strange land,
And fervently implored that a savior come to them.

Mother:

> Like our dear Lady, and also like her,
> Suddenly an unforeseen fate befell you.

Esther:

> The king's messengers traveled throughout the land
> To look for the most beautiful bride for the king.
> I was called to the palace before I knew it.
> The eye of the Lord fell on the poor maidservant.

Mother:

> When I read of it in the Book of Books,
> My heart became so heavy that it seemed to me
> I saw your soul full of deep pain
> And unshed tears.

Esther:

> It was hard indeed.
> Yet it was God's will, and I remained
> The poor maidservant of the Lord at the king's palace.
> My faithful uncle followed after me.
> He often came to the palace's door and brought news
> Of our people's needs and danger.
> So there came the day when I approached the king
> To plead for rescue from the deadly enemy.
> Life or death hung on his gaze.
> I leaned on the shoulders of my maid.
> But I was not alarmed before my husband's wrath.
> The eye that met mine was entirely friendly.
> In full favor, he handed me the scepter.
> Then my spirit was borne out of time and place.
> High in the clouds there was another throne,
> On which sits the Lord of Lords, before whom pales
> The earthly lord's vain glory.
> He himself, the Eternal, bowed down
> And promised me the salvation of my people.
> I sank down before the throne of the Highest as though dead.
> I found myself again in the arms of my husband.
> He addressed me lovingly and said that any wish—
> Whatever it might be—he would grant to me.
> This is how the highest Lord freed his people
> Through Esther, his maidservant, from the hands of Haman.

Mother:

>And today another Haman
>Has sworn to annihilate them in bitter hate.
>Is this in fact why Esther has returned?

Esther:

>You're the one who says so—
>Yes, I am traveling through the world
>To plead for lodgings for the homeless,
>The people so scattered and trampled
>That still cannot die.

Mother:

>How unusual!
>Don't you die as other people die?
>Were you carried off like Elijah
>Who, as people say, also wanders as a pilgrim?

Esther:

>I died a human death, was buried
>With royal pomp; but an angel accompanied
>My soul, its guardian,
>To the place of peace; it found its rest
>in Abraham's bosom with its ancestors.

Mother:

>In the bosom of Abraham—like Lazarus?

Esther:

>Like all who faithfully have served the Lord
>As their ancestors did. We waited there in peace,
>Still far from the light, so always in longing.
>But there came a day when, through all of creation,
>There occurred a fissure. All the elements seemed
>To be in revolt, night enveloped
>The world at noon. But in the midst of the night
>There stood, as if illumined by lightning, a barren mountain,
>And on the mountain a cross on which someone hung
>Bleeding from a thousand wounds; a thirst came over us
>To drink ourselves well from this fountain of wounds.
>The cross vanished into night, yet our night
>Was suddenly penetrated by a new light,
>Of which we had never had any idea: a sweet, blessed light.
>It streamed from the wounds of that man

Who had just died on the cross; now he stood
In our midst. He himself was the light,
The eternal light, that we had longed for from of old,
The Father's reflection and the salvation of the people.
He spread his arms wide and spoke
With a voice full of heavenly timbre:
Come to me all you who have faithfully served
The Father and lived in hope
Of the redeemer; see, he is with you,
He fetches you home to his Father's kingdom.
What happened then, there are no words to describe.
All of us who had awaited blessedness,
We were now at our goal—in the heart of Jesus.

Mother:

That's enough, or my heart will break
In longing for such great blessedness.
But no—speak further, speak of the homeland!

Esther:

Now in the mirror of eternal clarity, I saw
What happened after that on earth.
I saw the church grow out of my people,
A tenderly blooming sprig, saw that her heart was
The unblemished, pure shoot of David.
I saw flowing down from Jesus' heart
The fullness of grace into the Virgin's heart.
From there it flows to the members as the stream of life.
And again there came a day when she, the Blessed One
Was borne on high by a choir of angels
Up to the throne of the Almighty.
Her head was adorned with a crown of stars
And like the sun she was bathed in heavenly light.
But now I knew that I was bound to her
From eternity in accordance with God's direction—forever.
My life was only a beam of hers.

Mother:

And you left this blessed light
To tread the paths of earth again?

Esther:

That is her will, and mine as well.
The church had blossomed, but the masses

Of the people remained distant, far from the Lord
And his mother, enemies of the cross.
The people are in confusion and cannot find rest,
An object of disdain and scorn:
It will be thus until the final battle.
But before the cross appears again in heaven,
Even before Elijah comes to gather his own,
The good Shepherd goes silently through the lands.
Now and then he gathers from the depths of the abyss
A little lamb, shelters it at his heart.
And then others always follow him.
But there above at the throne of grace
The Mother ceaselessly pleads for her people.
She seeks souls to help her pray.
Then only when Israel has found the Lord,
Only then when he has received his own,
Will he come in manifest glory.
And we must pray for this second coming.

Mother:

Like once the first—I understand exactly.
You were the pathfinder for the first coming.
Now you are clearing the way to the kingdom of glory.
You came to me—do I now understand the message?
The Queen of Carmel sent you.
Where else was she to find hearts prepared
If not in her quiet sanctuary?
Her people, which are yours: your Israel,
I'll take it up into the lodgings of my heart.
Praying secretly and sacrificing secretly,
I'll take it home to my Savior's heart.

Esther:

You have understood, and so I can depart.
I am sure the guest will not be forgotten
Who came to you at the hour of midnight.
We'll meet again on the great day,
The day of manifest glory,
When above the head of the Queen of Carmel
The crown of stars will gleam brilliantly,
Because the twelve tribes will have found their Lord.
Farewell!

# Closing Hymn: Two Poems

### *Ich bleibe bei euch…*

Du thronest an des Vaters rechter Hand
im Reiche seiner ew'gen Herrlichkeit
als Gottes Wort von Anbeginn.

Du herrschest auf dem allerhöchsten Thron
auch in verklärter menschlicher Gestalt,
seitdem vollbracht dein Erdenwerk.

So glaube ich, weil es dein Wort mich lehrt,
und weil ich glaube, weiß ich es beglückt,
und sel'ge Hoffnung draus erblüht:

Denn wo du bist, da sind die Deinen auch,
der Himmel ist men herrlich Vaterland,
ich teil' mit dir des Vaters Thron.

Der Ewige, der alle Wesen schuf,
der, dreimal heilig, alles Sein umfaßt,
hat noch ein eig'nes stilles Reich.

Der Menschenseele innerstes Gemach
ist des Dreifalt'gen liebster Aufenthalt,
sein Himmelthron im Erdenland.

Dies Himmelreich aus Feindes Hand zu lösen,
ist Gottes Sohn als Menschensohn gekommen,
er gab sein Blut als Lösepreis.

134

### *I Will Remain With You...*

You reign at the Father's right hand
In the kingdom of his eternal glory
As God's Word from the beginning.

You reign on the Almighty's throne
Also in transfigured human form,
Ever since the completion of your work on earth.

I believe this because your word teaches me so,
And because I believe, I know it gives me joy,
And blessed hope blooms forth from it.

For where you are, there also are your own,
Heaven is my glorious homeland,
I share with you the Father's throne.

The Eternal who made all creatures,
Who, thrice holy, encompasses all being,
In addition has a silent, special kingdom of his own.

The innermost chamber of the human soul
Is the Trinity's favorite place to be,
His heavenly throne on earth.

To deliver this heavenly kingdom from the hand of the enemy,
The Son of God has come as Son of Man,
He gave his blood as the price of deliverance.

Im Herzen Jesu, das durchstochen ward,
sind Himmelreich und Erdenland verbunden,
hier is für uns des Lebens Quell.

Dies Herz ist der Dreifalt'gen Gottheit Herz
und aller Menschenherzen Mittelpunkt,
das uns der Gottheit Leben spendet.

Es zieht uns an sich mit geheimer Macht,
es birgt in sich uns in des Vaters Schoß
und strömt uns zu den Heil'gen Geist.

Dies Herz, es schlägt für uns im kleinen Zelt,
wo es geheimnisvoll verborgen weilt
in jenem stillen, weißen Rund.

Das ist dein Königsthron, o Herr, auf Erden,
den sichtbar du für uns errichtet hast,
und gerne siehst du mich ihm nah'n.

Du senkst voll Liebe deinen Blick in meinen
und neigst den Ohr zu meinen leisen Worten
und füllst mit Frieden tief das Herz.

Doch deine Liebe findet kein Genügen
in diesem Austausch, der noch Trennung läßt:
dein Herz verlangt nach mehr.

Du kommst als Frühmahl zu mir jeden Morgen.
Dein Fleisch und Blut wird mir zu Trank und Speise
und Wunderbares wird gewirkt.

Dein Leib durchdringt geheimnisvoll den meinen,
und deine Seele eint sich mit der meinen:
Ich bin nicht mehr, was einst ich war.

Du kommst und gehst, doch bleibt zurüch die Saat,
die du gesät zu künft'ger Herrlichkeit
verborgen in dem Leib von Staub.

Es bleibt ein Glanz des Himmels in der Seele,
es bleibt ein tiefes Leuchten in den Augen,
ein Schweben in der Stimme Klang.

In the heart of Jesus, which was pierced,
The kingdom of heaven and the land of earth are bound together.
Here is for us the source of life.

This heart is the heart of the triune Divinity,
And the center of all human hearts
That bestows on us the life of God.

It draws us to itself with secret power,
It conceals us in itself in the Father's bosom
And floods us with the Holy Spirit.

This Heart, it beats for us in a small tabernacle
Where it remains mysteriously hidden
In that still, white host.

That is your royal throne on earth, O Lord,
Which visibly you have erected for us,
And you are pleased when I approach it.

Full of love, you sink your gaze into mine
And bend your ear to my quiet words
And deeply fill my heart with peace.

Yet your love is not satisfied
With this exchange that could still lead to separation:
Your heart requires more.

You come to me as early morning's meal each daybreak.
Your flesh and blood become food and drink for me
And something wonderful happens.

Your body mysteriously permeates mine
And your soul unites with mine:
I am no longer what once I was.

You come and go, but the seed
That you sowed for future glory, remains behind
Buried in this body of dust.

A luster of heaven remains in the soul,
A deep glow remains in the eyes,
A soaring in the tone of voice.

Es bleibt das Band, das Herz mit Herz verbindet,
der Lebensstrom, der aus dem Deinen quillt
und jedes Glied belebt.

Wie wunderbar sind deiner Liebe Wunder,
wir staunen nur und stammeln und verstummen,
weil Geist und Wort versagt.

There remains the bond that binds heart to heart,
The stream of life that springs from yours
And animates each limb.

How wonderful are your gracious wonders!
All we can do is be amazed and stammer and fall silent
Because intellect and words fail.

### Und ich bleibe bei euch:
### Aus einer Pfingstnovene

1. Wer bist du süßes Licht, das mich erfüllt
und meines Herzens Dunkelheit erleuchtet?
Du leitest mich gleich einer Mutter Hand,
und ließest du mich los,
so wüßte keinen Schritt ich mehr zu gehen.
Du bist der Raum,
der rund mein Sein umschließt und in sich birgt.
Aus dir entlassen entsänk' es in den Abgrund
des Nichts, aus dem du es zum Licht erhobst.
Du, näher mir als ich mir selbst
und innerlicher als mein Innerstes
und doch untastbar und unfaßbar
und jeden Namen sprengend:
Heiliger Geist—ewige Liebe!

2. Bist du das süße Manna nicht,
das aus des Sohnes Herzen
in mein Herz überströmt,
der Engel und der Sel'gen Speise?
Er, der vom Tod zum Leben sich erhob,
er hat auch mich zu neuem Leben auferweckt
vom Schlaf des Todes.
Und neues Leben gibt er mir von Tag zu Tag,
und einst soll seine Fülle mich durchfluten,
Leben von deinem Leben—ja du selbst:
Heiliger Geist—ewiges Leben!

3. Bist du der Strahl,
der von des ew'gen Richters Thron herniederzuckt
und einbricht in die Nacht der Seele,
die nie sich selbst erkannt?
Barmherzig—unerbittlich
dringt er in verborg'ne Falten.

### And I Remain With You:
### From a Pentecost Novena

1. Who are you, sweet light, that fills me
And illumines the darkness of my heart?
You lead me like a mother's hand,
And should you let go of me,
I would not know how to take another step.
You are the space
That embraces my being and buries it in yourself.
Away from you it sinks into the abyss
Of nothingness, from which you raised it to the light.
You, nearer to me than I to myself
And more interior than my most interior
And still impalpable and intangible
And beyond any name:
Holy Spirit—eternal love!

2. Are you not the sweet manna
That from the Son's heart
Overflows into my heart,
The food of angels and the blessed?
He who raised himself from death to life,
He has also awakened me to new life
From the sleep of death.
And he gives me new life from day to day,
And at some time his fullness is to stream through me,
Life of your life—indeed, you yourself:
Holy Spirit—eternal life!

3. Are you the ray
That flashes down from the eternal Judge's throne
And breaks into the night of the soul
That had never known itself?
Mercifully—relentlessly
It penetrates hidden folds.

Erschreckt vom Anblick ihrer selbst
gewährt sie Raum heiliger Furcht,
dem Anfang jener Weisheit,
die aus der Höhe kommt
und in der Höhe uns fest verankert
*deinem* Wirken,
das neu uns schafft:
Heiliger Geist—alldurchdringender Strahl!

4. Bist du des Geistes Fülle und der Kraft,
womit das Lamm die Siegel löst
von Gottes ew'gem Ratschluß?
Von dir getrieben
reiten des Gerichtes Boten durch die Welt
und scheiden mit scharfem Schwert
das Reich des Lichtes von dem Reich der Nacht.
Dann wird der Himmel neu und neu die Erde,
und alles kommt an seinen rechten Ort
durch deinen Hauch:
Heiliger Geist—siegende Kraft!

5. Bist du der Meister, der den ew'gen Dom erbaut,
der von der Erde durch die Himmel ragt?
Von dir belebt erheben sich die Säulen hoch empor
und stehen unverrückbar fest.
Bezeichnet mit dem Ew'gen Namen Gottes
recken sie sich auf ins Licht,
die Kuppel tragend,
die den heil'gen Dom bekrönend abschließt,
dein weltumspannendes Werk:
Heiliger Geist—Gottes bildende Hand!

6. Bist du es, der den klaren Spiegel schuf,
zunächst des Allerhöchsten Thron,
gleich einem Meere von Kristall,
darin die Gottheit liebend sich beschaut?
Du neigst dich über deiner Schöpfung schönstes Werk,
und strahlend leuchtet dir
dein eig'ner Glanz entgegen.
Und aller Wesen reine Schönheit
vereinigt in der lieblichen Gestalt
der Jungfrau, deiner makellosen Braut:
Heiliger Geist—Schöpfer des All!

Alarmed at seeing itself,
The self makes space for holy fear,
The beginning of that wisdom
That comes from on high
And anchors us firmly in the heights,
Your action
That creates us anew:
Holy Spirit—ray that penetrates everything!

4. Are you the spirit's fullness and the power
By which the Lamb releases the seal
Of God's eternal decree?
Driven by you
The messengers of judgment ride through the world
And separate with a sharp sword
The kingdom of light from the kingdom of night.
Then heaven becomes new and new the earth,
And all finds its proper place
Through your breath:
Holy Spirit—victorious power!

5. Are you the master who builds the eternal cathedral,
Which towers from the earth through the heavens?
Animated by you, the columns are raised high
And stand immovably firm.
Marked with the eternal name of God,
They stretch up to the light,
Bearing the dome
That crowns the holy cathedral,
Your work that encircles the world:
Holy Spirit—God's molding hand!

6. Are you the one who created the unclouded mirror
Next to the Almighty's throne,
Like a crystal sea,
In which Divinity lovingly looks at itself?
You bend over the fairest work of your creation,
And radiantly your own gaze
Is illumined in return.
And of all creatures the pure beauty
Is joined in one in the dear form
Of the Virgin, your immaculate bride:
Holy Spirit—Creator of all!

7. Bist du das süße Lied der Liebe
und der heil'gen Scheu,
das ewig tönt um des Dreifaltigen Thron,
das aller Wesen reinen Klang in sich vermählt?
Der Einklang,
der zum Haupt die Glieder fügt,
darin ein jeder
seines Seins geheimnisvollen Sinn beseligt findet
und jubelnd ausströmt,
frei gelöst in deinem Strömen:
Heiliger Geist—ewiger Jubel!

7. Are you the sweet song of love
And of holy awe
That eternally resounds around the triune throne,
That weds in itself the clear chimes of each and every being?
The harmony,
That joins together the members to the Head,
In which each one
Finds the mysterious meaning of being blessed
And joyously surges forth,
Freely dissolved in your surging:
Holy Spirit—eternal jubilation!

# *NOTES*

**Preface**
1. [Available in English as *Essays on Woman*, trans. Freda Mary Oben, vol. 2 of *The Collected Works of Edith Stein* (Washington, DC: ICS Publications, 1987).—Tr.]

**Editor's Introduction**
1. Cf. *Edith Steins Werke*, vol. X, pp. 104, 140, 144.
2. Cf. Alfons P. Verbist, *L'affectivité: La fondamentale dans l'harmonie psychique* (Paris: Béatrice-Nauwelaerts, 1974), pp. 130ff.
3. Compare citations and presentations in this volume, Section II.4, with sayings in *Edith Steins Werke*, vol. VIII, p. 40 and vol. X, p. 144.
4. See sections III and IV and the last poem in this volume.
5. This turning of Edith Stein to the life of a religious, which is evident without being verbalized in "Love For Love," the reader will find presented in detail in *Edith Steins Werke*, vol. X, ch. III, pp. 30-49.
6. See *Edith Steins Werke*, vol. I, p. 282, footnote 2; see also vol. V, p. XIX.
7. Many thanks to the Mother Prioress and the other sisters.
8. [Edith Stein consistently used the blank side of letters, etc. for her notes and summaries.—Tr.]
9. We thank the tireless investigations of Sr. Maria Amata Neyer, O.C.D., Cologne, for a virtually complete list of these lectures that Edith Stein gave on two successive lecture tours in the years 1930-1932.
10. As a contribution to E. Lense, *Die in Deinem Hause wohnen* [*"Those Who Live in Your House"*] (Einsiedeln: Benziger), vol. II. In 1938, in the first volume of this collection, there appeared a biography written by Edith Stein: "A German Woman and Great Carmelite. Mother Franciska of the Infinite Merits of Jesus Christ, O.C.D. (Katharina Esser), 1814-1866."
11. We are talking about the following manuscripts:
—DI 14 *For January 6, 1941 (see below)*;
—DI 8 *Three Kings*, a clear presentation about following Christ and divine virtues, already written in the Dutch language by Edith Stein for the other sisters and novices. The manuscript is unpublished.

12. It has already been mentioned that there is another photocopy in handwriting and a typewritten transcript by Mother Johanna in the archives in the Cologne Carmel: a name-day piece for Mother Antonia from the year 1942. The stage setting is even written by Sister Benedicta in Dutch.

## On the History and Spirit of Carmel

1. [See St. Thérèse of Lisieux, *Story of a Soul* (Washington, DC: ICS Publications, 1976).—Tr.]

2. Gertrud von le Fort, *Die Letzte am Schafott* (Munich: Kösel, 1931). [Available in English as *The Song at the Scaffold*, trans. Olga Marx (New York, NY: Sheed and Ward, 1933)—Tr.]

3. Idem, Foreword to Marie Antoinette de Geuser's *Briefe in dem Karmel [Letters in Carmel]*, (Regensberg, Munich: Pustet, 1934).

4. Cf. Erik Peterson, "Theologie des Kleides" ["Theology of Clothing"], *Benediktinische Monatscrift* 9/10 (1934), p. 354.

5. For the liturgical texts, cf. *Die Eigenmessen der Unbeschuhten Karmeliten [The Proper Masses of the Discalced Carmelites]*, (Linz: Verlag Skapulier, out of print).

6. *Regel und Satzungen der unbeschuhten Nonnen des Ordens der Allerseligsten Jungfrau Maria vom Berge Karmel [Rule and Constitutions of the Discalced Nuns of the Order of the Most Blessed Virgin Mary of Mount Carmel]* (Würzburg: Rita-Verlag, 1928).

7. [The writings of St. Teresa of Jesus are available in English as *The Collected Works of St. Teresa of Avila*, trans. Kieran Kavanaugh and Otilio Rodriguez, 3 vols. (Washington, DC: ICS Publications, 1976-1987)—Tr.]

8. [The writings of St. John of the Cross are available in English in *The Collected Works of St. John of the Cross*, trans. Kieran Kavanaugh and Otilio Rodriguez, rev. ed. (Washington, DC: ICS Publications, 1991), as well as in a number of other editions.—Tr.]

## The Prayer of the Church

1. Judaism had and has its richly formed liturgy for public as well as for family worship, for feast days and for ordinary days.

2. "Praise to you, our Eternal God, King of the Universe, who brings forth bread from the earth...who creates the fruit of the vine."

3. Mt 26:26-28.

4. For example, before awakening Lazarus (Jn 11:41-42).

5. Cf. N. Glatzer and L. Strauß, *Sendung und Schicksal: Aus dem Schriftum des nachbiblischen Judentums [Mission and Fate: From the Writings of Post-Biblical Judaism]* (Berlin: Schocken-Verlag, 1931), pp. 2ff.

6. Erik Peterson in *Buch von dem Engeln [Book of the Angels]* (Leipzig: Verlag Hegner, 1935) has shown in an unsurpassed way the union of the

heavenly and earthly Jerusalem in the celebration of the liturgy. [This work is available in English as *The Angels and the Liturgy*, trans. Ronald Walls (New York, NY: Herder & Herder, 1964).—Tr.]

7. Naturally, it is a prerequisite that one is not burdened with serious sins; otherwise, one could not receive Holy Communion "in the proper spirit."

8. Mt 4:1-2.

9. Lk 6:12.

10. Lk 22:42.

11. Jn 13:1.

12. Jn 17.

13. Lv 16:17.

14. Lv 16:16.

15. Lv 16:13.

16. Because the limits of this essay do not permit me to cite Jesus' entire high priestly prayer, I must ask readers to take up St. John's Gospel at this point and re-read chapter 17.

17. Acts 9.

18. Acts 10.

19. *The Way of Perfection*, in *Schriften der heiligen Teresa von Jesus*, vol. 2, ch. 1 (Regensberg, 1907). [English translation in *The Collected Works of St. Teresa of Avila*, trans. Kieran Kavanaugh and Otilio Rodriguez, vol. 2, (Washington, DC: ICS Publications, 1980), ch. 1, sec. 1 and 5, pp. 41 and 42.—Tr.]

20. *The Way of Perfection*, ch. 3. Both of these passages are regularly read in our Order on Ember Days [in Edith Stein's time—Tr.].

21. *Interior Castle*, Seventh Dwelling Place, ch 2, sec. 1. [Also contained in *The Collected Works of St. Teresa of Avila*, trans. Kavanaugh and Rodriguez, vol. 2 (Washington, DC: ICS Publications, 1980)—Tr.]

22. Rom 8:26.

23. 1 Cor 12:3.

24. Marie de la Trinité, *Lettres de "Consummata" à une Carmélite* (Carmel d'Avignon, 1930), letter of September 27, 1917. Published in German as *Briefe in den Karmel* (Regensberg: Pustet, 1934), pp. 263ff. [See also Raoul Plus, *Consummata: Marie Antoinette de Geuser, her Life and Letters*, English edition by George Baker (New York, NY: Benziger, 1931).—Tr.]

25. "There is one interior adoration...adoration in Spirit, which abides in the depths of human nature, in its understanding and in its will; it is authentic, superior adoration, without which outer adoration remains without life." From *"O mein Gott, Dreifalitger, den ich anbete": Gebet der Schwester Elisabeth von der Heligisten Dreifaltigkeit ["O My God, Trinity Whom I Adore": Prayer of Sister Elizabeth of the Trinity]*, interpreted by Dom Eugene Vandeur, OSB (Regensburg, 1931), p. 23. [English translation:

*Trinity Whom I Adore,* trans. Dominican Nuns of Corpus Christi Monastery (New York, NY: Pustet, 1953).—Tr.]

26. [There are oblique references in this sentence to the Carmelite *Rule* and to St. Thérèse, who said she wished to be love in the heart of the church.—Tr.]

27. St. Augustine, "Tract. 27 in Joannem," from the Roman Breviary [of Edith Stein's day—Tr.], readings 8 and 9 of the third day in the octave of Corpus Christi.

28. Loc. cit., St. John Chrysostom, "Homily 61 to the people of Antioch," fourth reading.

29. Roman Missal [of Edith Stein's day-Tr.], Postcommunion for the first Sunday after Pentecost.

**The Spirit of St. Elizabeth as It Informed Her Life**

1. [The region in east central Germany, including the Thuringia Forest near the Czech border.—Tr.]

2. Heinrich von Kleist, *Über das Marionettentheater.* [An English translation by Cherna Murray, under title "About the Marionette Theater," can be found in *Life and Letters Today* 16 (Summer, 1957).—Tr.]

**Life and Work of St. Teresa of Jesus**

1. [In fact, recent studies have shown that Teresa was of Jewish ancestry; see Teofanes Egido, "The Historical Setting of St. Teresa's Life," *Carmelite Studies* 1 (1980): 122-182. Throughout this essay, Edith Stein writes in light of the historical data available to her at the time. Some minor corrections (of dates, etc.) have been inserted into the text of this translation, but the basic presentation remains as she wrote it.—Tr.]

2. [According to recent research, the dedication of the chapel of the Monastery of the Incarnation took place in the same year (1515) as Teresa's birth, but not on the same day; see Efrén de la Madre de Dios and Otger Steggink, *Tiempo y Vida de Santa Teresa,* 2d ed. *(Madrid: Biblioteca de Autores Cristianos, 1977),* pp. 22-25, 90.—Tr.]

3. [Throughout this essay, to help preserve its original flavor, citations of St. Teresa's works have been translated directly from the comparatively free German translation that Edith Stein used. In addition, for the convenience of the reader, we have inserted cross-references (in brackets) to the ICS translations of the same texts, whenever these could be located. The latter may be found in *The Collected Works of St. Teresa of Avila,* trans. Kieran Kavanaugh and Otilio Rodriguez, vols. 1-3 (Washington, DC: ICS Publications, 1976-1985). The following system of abbreviations is used: F = *Book of Foundations;* L = *Book of Her Life;* C = *Interior Castle;* W = *Way of Perfection;* ST = *Spiritual Testimonies.* Ordinarily, the two numbers following the initial letter indicate chapter and section,

respectively; for the *Interior Castle*, however, the firstnumber indicates the "dwelling place." Thus, "C, 1, 2, 3" refers to the third section of the second chapter in the first "dwelling places" of the *Interior Castle.*—Tr.]

4. According to the saint. Fourteen in the latest research. [Ed.]

5. In particular in her *Life, Way of Perfection,* and *Interior Castle.* The references cited so far are from her *Life.* However, it is recommended that the reader who has not yet dealt with spiritual writings begin with the *Way of Perfection.* The presentation of the Our Father contained in it is a model example of contemplative prayer.

6. Oettingen-Spieberg, *Geschichte der hl. Teresia* [*Biography of St. Teresa*], Regensberg: Habbel, vol. I, p. 313f.

7. Probably an error by Edith Stein. The provincial at that time was Fr. Gregorio Fernández (1559-1561). Fr. Angel de Salazar was prior in Avila in 1541. He was provincial from 1551-1553. [Ed.]

8. It is said that our Holy Mother at first wore only sandals that left the feet uncovered, as our friars still do today. It was when her dainty feet were admired once during a trip that she introduced [leggings with the] hempen sandals called "alpargatas." [Ed.]

9. See note 7. [Ed.]

10. After she had discovered and tested the most appropriate regimen in living with her daughters, she wrote her "Constitutions," which—except for a few minor changes—today continue to contain the valid rules of her Order. They are contained in her writings. [See *Collected Works of St. Teresa,* vol. 3, pp. 319-333.—Tr.]

11. See note 7. [Ed.]

12. *Interior Castle,* seventh dwelling places, chap. 3. [The text does not appear in precisely this form in the ICS translation.—Tr.]

13. A learned Augustinian who published the first printed edition of Teresa's writings (1588).

14. At her death Teresa left behind fourteen monasteries of the reform for men and sixteen for women. Soon thereafter the Order spread to France. Today it is established all over the world. A great number of lay people are united with it by the Secular Order and the Scapular Fraternity. The Teresian Prayer Organization (at the Carmelite Monastery in Würzburg) assembles everyone who wants to intercede for the needs of the Holy Church and the Holy Father into a great prayer army, and lets them participate in all the good works of the Carmelite Order.

### A Chosen Vessel of Divine Wisdom: Sr. Marie-Aimée de Jésus

1. *Soeur Marie-Aimée de Jésus, Religieuse Carmélite… (d'après ses notes),* 2 vols., 1923; *N.S. Jésus-Christ, étudié dans las saint Évangile: Sa vie dâns l'âme fidele,* 6 vols., 1922-1924. Both books are published by the Carmel of the Avenue de Saxe, which has now moved to Créteil near Paris.

2. *Soeur Marie-Aimée de Jésus...*, vol. 1, p. 9f.

3. The second, a little sister, was sent to the country to try to keep her alive. She died shortly after the mother.

4. Ibid., vol. 1, p. 46.

5. Ibid., vol. 1, p. 194.

6. Ibid., vol. 1, p. 194f.

7. Cf. the German translation, *Die zwölf Grade des Schweigens* ["The Twelve Levels of Silence"], by Sister M. Amata of Jesus, Discalced Carmelite (Dülmen i.W: Verlag Laumann, 1937).

8. *Sr. Marie-Aimée de Jésus,* vol. 1, p. 237.

9. Ibid., vol. 1, p. 309ff.

10. Ibid., vol. 1, p. 314.

11. Ibid., vol. 1, p. 416.

12. *N.S. Jésus-Christ,* vol. II, p. 422.

**For the First Profession of Sr. Miriam of Little St. Thérèse**
1. This was the customary form of address used among the Discalced Carmelite nuns before Vatican II. [Ed.]

**The Hidden Life and Epiphany**
1. In 1940, January 6 fell on a Saturday. [Ed.]

**For January 6, 1941**
1. At that time, every Mass ended with the prologue of John's Gospel. [Ed.]

**I Am Always in Your Midst**
1. [St. Angela Merici was an Italian religious who founded the Ursuline Order (1535) who died in 1540.—Tr.]

**Conversations at Night**
1. [The "turn," where visitors ring the bell, is at the entrance of the monastery. —Tr.]

# INDEX

153

The Institute of Carmelite Studies promotes research and publication in the field of Carmelite spirituality. Its members are Discalced Carmelites, part of a Roman Catholic community—friars, nuns and laity—who are heirs to the teaching and way of life of Teresa of Jesus and John of the Cross, men and women dedicated to contemplation and to ministry in the Church and the world. Information concerning their way of life is available through local diocesan Vocation Offices, or from the Vocation Director's Office, 1525 Carmel Road, Hubertus, WI 53033.